Preface

Monsieur Martin, frequently in a state of semi-undress, drives past Phyllida's house on his tractor most days. He lives down the lane with his short wife, an impressive number of small speckled ponies that are often accompanied by several attendant Little Egrets, and a dog that begins to bark every evening just as the aperitif arrives in the neighbours' garden.

The ponies are of a miniature variety; their purpose is unspecified save to make more spotted ponies which can then be sold to someone who may also be of restricted growth. And the dog is a nasty but unfortunate creature that belongs to a son who keeps him locked in a shed. Madame Martin never steps outside the front or back doors of the house which her husband constructed for her security. Madame Martin is a recluse: badly treated as a child, she was forced to assume a position of disproportionate responsibility as the bottom prop in a large family of acrobats.

She was rescued by Monsieur Martin who, as a younger man, happened to pass a summer in the big top with a troupe of performing poodles. Madame Martin, despite being afraid of dogs, was, nonetheless, swept off her tiny feet by promises of a new life wherein canvas was replaced by bricks, and poodles substituted with small ponies; in a place where she could get everyone off her back. However, history doesn't shed its load so easily; which is why, according to Monsieur Martin, his wife spends her hot Provençal days inside the house. Apparently, she passes her time making confiture from the various ingredients which her husband grows in the garden that she only views occasionally through a grimy window.

Madame Martin has a bad back: the weight of her family caused this disability. She finds it difficult to walk and, never a tall woman in the first place, she has, apparently, shrunk in size; and continues to do so. Perhaps marrying a woman who is vertically challenged is what inspired the half-naked, but not unsympathetic, Monsieur Martin to invest in a selection of equally small ponies. Possibly, it was a thoughtful attempt to lessen her feelings of torment caused by a larger world; although why he married such a woman when the only possible benefit was a constant supply of home-made jam is unclear.

When not in the kitchen, Madame Martin likes to watch television, especially with her son, Christophe. The son departs at an early hour to pack potatoes into sacks somewhere or other and returns home to spend the rest of the day indoors watching French TV with his mother. To my mind, there's not much difference between the entertainment value of a sack of potatoes and French TV but, each to their own. There's little in the way of alternative entertainment in the tiny hamlet of Cabannes. Still, it can't be easy for Monsieur Martin who, having saved his wife from an overbearing family and fulfilling all his promises, has little to shout about apart from a spoonful of home-made Reine Claudes every now and then with his breakfast. This is probably why he was so keen on Sophy.

Sophy, who was once Christophe's girlfriend, also lived down the lane. Monsieur Martin liked her very much in a paternal sort of way. This was largely due to the fact that she didn't make jam and had no interest in French television; preferring to be outside in the Provençal sunshine with the semi-naked Monsieur Martin, the small speckled ponies and the Little Egrets. Sadly, this happy companionship had no future. Sophy was also shrinking.

It was difficult to say when it began – more a question of Monsieur Martin suddenly noticing one day how much weight Sophy had lost. He sent her off to Noves to see young Doctor Giraud, a man as slight in stature as to seem of little consequence. The good doctor promptly prescribed a course of medication entirely without efficacy. Sophy refused to gain any weight and became smaller and smaller. No amount of Monsieur Martin's home-grown, oddly shaped, but uniquely tasty tomatoes, and aubergines as crooked as a French politician, could adequately sustain the young woman. Surprisingly, his enormous courgettes also appeared to be nutritionally deficient. Even the sun-soaked natural sweetness of Madame Martin's confiture held no obvious redeeming properties. For Monsieur Martin, the situation was une catastrophe: Sophy, who was also

CHEZ MARTIN

MADAME VERTE

decreasing in height, became too tiny to help with the ponies and Monsieur Martin was eventually forced to reduce the herd. In number that is.

For a whole year, under her caring father-in-law's supervision, Sophy continued to visit Doctor Giraud until, one day, the ever-diminishing young woman disappeared completely. Like Madame Martin, who had yet to vanish into oblivion, Sophy was not seen in public again; her disappearance unnoticed by two of the three who lived down the lane. Unlike Madame Martin, however, she was not ensconced in a darkened kitchen filling pots with jam or hidden away in front of television game shows designed for the small minded: she was recuperating in bed in Noves – with Doctor Giraud.

Gradually, with the kindly doctor's help, but sadly unknown to Monsieur Martin, Sophy regained her strength and general interest in life. Soon, she was seen out and about in the village; which is more than could ever be said for Madame Martin. One day, Sophy was even spotted jogging down the road to Cabannes where she paused briefly to look with some longing at the remaining small speckled ponies in the field. She didn't turn down the lane though. That way laid desolation where no-one was on top. Far more fun to be under the doctor.

Part One

Chapter One

The unpleasant dog that begins to bark every evening chez Martin, just as those in the surrounding neighbourhood are about to commence a tranquil aperitif, has a name. Given that the impoverished animal passes its Provençal days chained to a stump in the tiniest of enclosures behind the house, with only the company of similarly caged assorted livestock – rabbits, goats, chickens and so forth – it might seem unlikely that, at some point in its puppyhood, anyone had bothered to assign the dog nomenclature; or, if they had bothered, it seems inconceivable that they called it something other than 'arête' or 'putain', either of which can be heard drifting over the airwaves courtesy of the potato-packing, Pastis-swigging Christophe.

In fact, on the day the dog was given to Christophe, in lieu of some unknown, unpaid and irrelevant debt accrued in the PMU bar at Cabannes, the young man had just spent an hour watching a repeat of Who Wants to be a Millionaire? (he does) with his mother. During this riot of intellectualism, Christophe had learned that the first king of France was called Clovis. Feeling this to be a significant piece of information with which he might impress Sophy who, at that time, was still his girlfriend, he determined to store it within his working memory. Accordingly, and as an aide memoire, he gave the name Clovis to the unwanted wolf-puppy; although, in truth, by the time that Sophy left for the heady life in Noves, Christophe had long since forgotten why the dog was called Clovis. In the same way, he'd also forgotten that the dog even had a name. Madame Martin, however, had not forgotten.

Thus far, not much time has been allotted to Madame Martin: certainly not by Monsieur Martin once he had discovered she was a woman of the interior who, apparently, resisted the exterior benefits of living in Provence with relish and confiture. Not by Christophe either although, to be fair, he continued to pass his afternoons with Maman sharing her addiction to televised quiz shows. And, unfortunately, not by us. Thus, it falls to your narrator to remedy this error.

We know something of Madame's provenance: the youngest daughter of a large family of acrobats who, being dark and swarthy, may have originated in Italy or North Africa or some other dark and swarthy clime – Wales for example; oppressed and partially disabled by her position as bottom prop in the performing pyramid; more than adept in the jam and pickle department; and voluntarily confined to the house. In respect of the latter, albeit from choice, Madame Martin has an element of entrapment empathy with Clovis.

The tethered Clovis, grumbling through the day from dawn until the grumble reaches a crescendo of impotent barking in the late afternoon, is looking for some action. And so, although she is as yet unaware, is Madame Martin as she growls around the solitary confinement of her Provençal mornings, mixing fruit and boiling sugar. Apart from the back pain which has burdened her since childhood, and a touch of repetitive strain injury caused by the constant sieving of fruit and sugar, Madame's general health is good. Clovis, on the other hand, is wilting. He has lost his appetite. Madame Martin is worried by the loss of affection and size that comprises a constant theme in this household. She has heard of the dog's demise from her husband and demands that Monsieur Martin takes Clovis to see the vet at St. Remy.

Monsieur Martin is appalled at the suggestion. Between maintaining his decimated herd of small spotted ponies, worrying about the errant Sophy and irrigating his courgettes, there is, in his humble opinion, no time for such an extravagance as taking a dog on a certain-to-be expensive outing. Further, there is no-one to help him secure the unwieldy animal in his pick-up truck.

Madame is insistent: 'look what happened to Sophy', she argues. Monsieur Martin, although he doesn't say as much, would be secretly grateful if, like Sophy, Clovis disappeared. Neither does he think, (but also keeps his opinion to himself), that there's much chance of Clovis ending up in bed in Noves with Doctor Giraud which is what happened to Sophy. He hasn't shared this knowledge with either his wife or Christophe fearing that his son might also develop a sudden desire to see the medic.

It's the end of August by the time Monsieur Martin has finally been brow-beaten into submission. All of the fruit in the orchard has been harvested and Madame has her hands and jars full to the brim. The late spring developed into a summer that refuses to subside and the temperature has soared to 40C when Monsieur Martin wrestles Clovis into the truck on the last day of the month. During the previous hour, Clovis has experienced all the emotions a dog can possibly manage. He began with his usual abject desperation on waking to yet another day of imprisonment before settling into a well-practised sulk. When Monsieur Martin made an appearance with a stick, a rope and a collar, Clovis immediately fell into a state of complete shock. Monsieur Martin made the most of the dog's temporary collapse and had secured the collar and the rope before Clovis rallied and began to vent his anger at this uncalled for intrusion.

How Monsieur Martin and Clovis ended up together in the truck would be a matter of speculation discussed in local hostelries for many years to come. The dog may have been on hunger strike for a number of weeks but its efforts to resist an unexpected trip were valiant given his lethargy. The fight was reported to have been heard all over Cabannes and even reached Noves where the local gendarmerie entertained the notion of investigating the cause of the noise for at least five minutes. Monsieur Martin and Clovis, meanwhile, were sharing the bench seat in the truck, each in a state of total exhaustion, both missing tufts of hair and sporting a colourful array of injuries.

On reaching St Remy, Monsieur Martin was suddenly struck by the notion that there might be people inside the veterinary clinic with cats. Clovis was snoring loudly to his right but Monsieur Martin knew very well that there could be trouble ahead if cats were involved. What Monsieur Martin had not considered, never having been much of an adherent to either clocks or calendars, was that tomorrow was the first day of the season. The season of La Chasse. In the event, the vet's waiting room was empty of cats for the sole reason that every feline owner for miles knew that today was the day when, by the law of some authority or other, every hunting dog in Provence was obliged to undergo registration, examination, inoculation, and a number of other procedures too sordid to mention, in order that they could legally retrieve whatever their owners chose to shoot the following day.

Monsieur Martin drags Clovis across the car park. To begin with, the going is slow but, suddenly, Clovis picks up the scent of another dog; and another; and yet another. With so much requisite territorial marking, the starving animal proves surprisingly adept at a three – legged hop, skip and jump towards the clinic. By the time he arrives, Clovis has regained all his lost strength and is salivating in anticipation as Monsieur Martin opens the door to the surgery.

Inside, the place is positively heaving with Springer Spaniels of all colours and hues. Naturally excitable, but always friendly, the Springers momentarily freeze as Clovis, the wolf-dog, appears. Then, in a quantum leap from team-workers to pack, the Springers spring. Clovis bays and dives for the centre of the scrum. Madame, the receptionist, screams and takes cover under her desk. Otherwise calm and professional dog-rearing hunters discover language that was, even to them, hitherto unknown. Ropes are waved and sticks are struck as if some errant troupe of Morris dancers has stumbled into Provence. Vets arrive on this scene of carnage armed with hypodermic syringes and someone calls the pompiers.

Monsieur Martin, having committed to a heavier than anticipated vet's bill, eventually arrives chez lui with a dejected Clovis at 5 in the afternoon. Madame Martin is furious for a number of reasons; not least having been disturbed from the final of her favourite quiz in order to search for bandages and plasters. Christophe, sitting passively, promises to relay the outcome of the show. Clovis is reassigned to his enclosure. For half an hour, he lays quietly turning over the day's events in his mind. Then, on hearing the clink of glasses over in Phyllida's pleasant garden, he begins to bark.

Chapter Two

There has been a momentous turn of events chez Martin. Following the debacle at the veterinary surgery in St Remy, an account of which has been published in Le Dauphin, Monsieur Martin is refusing to have any further contact with Clovis. Christophe, who, let's be fair is the dog's legal guardian, is otherwise occupied. Having spent so many weeks, months, years even, watching inane quiz shows on daytime television, it has occurred to him that he might be in possession of more trivia than can be deemed good for a person. Or, put another way, more trivia that could be good for a person. Accordingly, he has decided to enter a team into a quiz night that has been organised at the bar-tabac in St Remy by a group of bored ex-pats. Therefore, if the dog is not to completely starve, it falls to Madame Martin to break the habit of a Provençal lifetime by going outside to feed Clovis. The alternatives are too shocking for consideration: either the dog will die or, even worse, must be brought into the kitchen.

Furthermore, even though the dog is in a weakened and sorry state, his barking is no longer constrained to that time of day when the aperitif is due. During the infamous Battle with the Springer Spaniels, Clovis discovered that he could bay and practises this new noise at all hours, interspersed with attempts to try, as yet, uncategorised alternatives: simpering, whimpering and howling to name, once accomplished, three.

Over on the other side of the orchard, Phyllida is not happy. Being a consummate animal lover, Phyllida doesn't mind the aperitif-accompanying barking. She feels sorry for the dog and the life it leads and finds a spot of doggie outpouring whilst sipping her Mojito almost ritualistic. De rigeur one might say. But not this incessant range of canine crying. It's almost unbearable and Phyllida is very close to her first ever experience of hating an animal.

However, Phyllida being Phyllida, finds it impossible to mention the problem to Monsieur Martin. She likes Monsieur Martin. She likes watching him pass by, semi-naked, on his tractor: it's all so - French. She likes enquiring after Madame Martin's health when Monsieur Martin calls to show her his courgettes. She likes this multicultural interaction so says nothing. Nonetheless, an air of unease hangs over the place like a Singapore Smog.

Clutching a tempting piece of best rump steak (that her husband will never see) to her apron clad breasts (which he also never sees), Madame Martin takes a tentative step outside the back door one evening.

'Mon Dieu', she thinks. 'When did it get this bad?'

It's true, of course, that Madame Martin is extremely small so even a normal sized shrubbery will appear as a veritable jungle. What greets her, however, is not that far removed from the sites she has previously and correctly identified in the geography section of her favourite quiz programme. In some places, the scorched earth resembles the dust bowls of the Hall of Africa; in other areas – notably those through which she now sets a course – the Amazon rain forest springs to mind.

Madame Martin returns to the kitchen and retrieves the bread knife in order to hack her way through the remains of her husband's rhubarb. Emerging finally through the undergrowth that has scratched her tiny arms to shreds, Madame Martin arrives at the cage in which Clovis, much like those over at Phyllida's place, is currently trying out a new whine.

To say the dog was startled would be an understatement. It was bad enough when Monsieur Martin turned up with the offer of a day out in St Remy, but to witness the appearance of Madame Martin is a shock too far. Clovis is immediately silenced; as are the dinner guests over at Phyllida's who have suddenly discovered themselves unnecessarily shouting at each other over the Pastis and peanuts. They look around then look at each other, trying to work out what has changed. Clovis, meanwhile, is looking at Madame Martin. Or, more precisely, at the piece of rump steak dangling from her jam encrusted fingers. Clovis has fallen in love. A bond is about to be formed.

Entering the dog's territory will be one giant step for womankind that Madame Martin is unwilling to take on this most auspicious of evenings. Instead, she attempts to insert the piece of steak through the mesh that separates her from the dog. It's a tricky procedure as Clovis, having yet to discover the concept of patience, is snapping at Madame's jammy hands, enthralled to discover that the plat du jour and desert have arrived simultaneously.

And this will continue for a week after which, Madame Martin reaches three conclusions: firstly, she now has a foliage-free pathway that exists between the back door and the dog's enclosure; secondly, she and the dog now share a mutual respect for each other that borders on friendship; and thirdly, despite eating every jam-covered delicacy that is squeezed into his cage, Clovis is still losing weight.

Monsieur Martin will not even discuss the viability of another visit to see the vet. Christophe has no time to consider such an outing being presently confined either in the potato packing centre or in the mediathèque in Avignon where he is preparing for his forthcoming appearance at the inaugural quiz show in St Remy. Madame Martin, making up for lost time, as she quickly evolves into another incarnation, bravely picks up the telephone and calls the veterinary surgery to demand a home visit.

With only two weeks left until the quiz evening in St Remy, Christophe is feeling confident of success and imminent fame. Every afternoon he is to be found in the mediathèque devouring the recipes of Escoffier, flags of French speaking colonies, departments of France, football teams of the French premier division and presidents of La République. In the evenings, he reads Pagnol, Flaubert and Daudet. For supper, he has started to demand fish to stimulate those areas of his Rip Van Winkle brain which have not yet awakened. As the fish van only arrives outside the Intermarché in Cabannes on Fridays, at a time when he is practising his French rivers and Impressionists down at the potato-packing centre, thus far, fish remains absent from his menu.

One evening, Christophe makes an unexpected discovery in what passes for the garden behind chez Martin. Busy reading Le Monde on the way to his own private privy, he stumbles over a small, unexpected obstacle on a newly formed path. It transpires that the small, unexpected obstacle is a tiny woman. It is Madame Martin returning from her nightly negotiations with Clovis. Once Christophe has overcome his shock at finding his mother on the wrong side of the kitchen door, it occurs to him that, having got this far, Maman might, for a change of scenery, try the other side of the front door. To be exact, she might as well pop down to Intermarché and get him some fish.

On hearing this suggestion, Madame Martin regards her son as if she has only just discovered that, some years ago, she gave birth to an imbecile.

'No chance', she retorts. 'I'm waiting in for the vet'.

The son looks at the mother carefully for the first time since he was an infant in her arms. There is something different about her. However, as whatever the difference is seems to have no obvious bearing on either the acquisition of fish or the forthcoming quiz, he dismisses the thought almost before it has become fully formed in a space reserved for the demise of Marie-Antoinette.

Madame Martin is indeed waiting for the arrival of the vet the following day. What she has not chosen to share with Christophe is that this will be the second visit of the week. When the call from chez Martin was received by the receptionist at the veterinary clinic on Tuesday, and when the receptionist had passed on the information to Monsieur Rivière, the owner of the surgery, and when Monsieur Rivière had shared the news with his two assistant vets, a combined degree of horror and panic ensued. At the time, they were still attempting to settle the insurance claim made subsequent to their previous encounter with Clovis, the wolf-dog. It was true that their agenda were full for the foreseeable future with repairs to an undisclosed number of Springer Spaniels. It was also true that the start of La Chasse in the St. Remy environs had, for the first time in living memory, and two weeks before that, been indefinitely postponed due to the unavailability of a sufficient number of hunting dogs replete with the full quota of body parts. This, in turn, had put the vets under even greater pressure to get on with the healing processes.

With combined bribery, the vets had managed to persuade some local carpenters and decorators to complete the renovation of the reception and waiting room areas in record time. Further, the vets had updated each other's tetanus inoculations and most of their wounds were now healing nicely. Nonetheless, there was no chance that any half sane person who had been in attendance during the first and only visit of Clovis would be rushing over chez Martin for another rendezvous.

Fortuitously, however, now that his leg was once again marginally usable, one of the assistant vets was due to spend two days in the Henri Duffaut hospital in Avignon for intensive physiotherapy. A locum was due up from Marseilles which, at a mere 90K, was the nearest point yet to hear the true reason for the rebuilding of the clinic at St. Remy.

'Send Monsieur Villiers', ordered Monsieur Rivière with what looked suspiciously like the hint of a smirk.

Monsieur Villiers, being currently from the port of Marseilles, but hitherto, like most in that place, of an unknown provenance that could have originated anywhere, was dark and swarthy. He was also extremely short. In fact, when he first appeared in the surgery, Madame, the receptionist, could only see his mop of tight black curls from the seat behind the desk and mistook him for a passing Standard Poodle who was late for his appointment. On checking his pedigree, Madame, the receptionist, welcomed Monsieur Villiers and immediately dispatched him to Cabannes, with, it has to be said, a degree of guilt-ridden regret: in their briefest of acquaintances, he'd seemed like quite a nice man really.

Monsieur Martin has, naturally, heard of the vet's impending visit; has, in fact, received news of this unexpected turn of events with more than a little surprise. However, being now under a life-time ban from the clinic at St. Remy, and having sworn to have nothing else to do with Clovis, unless it involves a shot-gun, Monsieur Martin merely instructs his wife not to part with any money:

'Pay him some other way – jam or pickle or something'.

Nonetheless, when Monsieur Villiers turns off the road between Cabannes and Noves and, heading down the lane, stops to admire the small spotted ponies, Monsieur Martin, being French, feels it only right and proper to exchange Bonjours. Monsieur Villiers remains in his car so his height, or lack of it, remains unnoticed by Monsieur Martin. In any case, it would have made little difference: Monsieur Martin is currently preoccupied having just spotted a diminutive and familiar figure jogging along the road towards Noves.

Monsieur Villiers makes his own way into the sweet smelling kitchen. Madame Martin has spent the morning boiling up the last of the Reine Claudes and both she and the kitchen have taken on the luminous hues sometimes associated with weak sunlight waging battle against a stagnant pond. Monsieur Villiers looks Madame Martin in the eyes – one of only a small minority who have ever accomplished this feat without kneeling - and tenderly brushes away a rogue piece of greengage skin from her cheek:

'Bonjour ma chérie'.

Monsieur Villiers has bypassed the grimy visage of Madame Martin and found the hidden, and largely unrecognised (up-until-this-point) mysterious beauty of the South. Madame, meanwhile, having experienced, and in this order, surprise at the unannounced arrival of her visitor, amazement at his greeting, astonishment at his height and never-for-years-seen colouring, horror at having her cheek touched so intimately and – yes- embarrassment at the state of her kitchen has, in short, been caught sur la hop. Finding herself devoid of anything apposite to say, she pulls herself up, for the first time in years, to her full height and says: 'Monsieur, this way to the dog s'il vous plait'.

She leads the veterinary locum down the once rhubarb infested pathway to the cage where Clovis, sleeping in the midday sun, finds an unexpected opportunity to show off his newly discovered snarl. Monsieur Villiers listens attentively to the brief history of devoured rump steak, minced venison and Meurgez sausages, during which all references to past events at the clinic in St. Remy are conspicuous by their absence. Monsieur Villiers writes a few notes in his moleskin covered notebook. He politely refuses an invitation to enter the dog's enclosure and meditates for few moments on the blue Provençal skies. Then he turns to Madame Martin and delivers his diagnosis:

'Madame, it is clearly a case of love starvation'.

Chapter Three

At the PMU bar in Cabannes, Christophe is generally considered to be making a nuisance of himself with his constant and tiresome efforts to recruit members to his quiz team. All initial attempts have been met with derision by the locals. Firstly, they argue, the thought of spending an evening answering general knowledge questions is not their idea of a good night out. Secondly, an expedition of 7K to St. Remy in order to spend an evening answering general knowledge questions is a joke. Thirdly, the idea of spending an evening in St. Remy answering general knowledge questions in the company of ex-pats is inconceivable. What could possibly be gained?

'80 euro and the infinite glory of beating the English and Americans at their own game', replies the wily Christophe as he digs deeper into his overall pockets for the price of another round of drinks.

The matter is reconsidered.

'We don't have any general knowledge', his friends argue, but Christophe begs to differ. He reminds them that Thiery knows everything there is to be known regarding the history of Les Bleus.

'Be fair, he even got Chabal's autograph in the 2007 cup'. And they have to agree that it's a fact; although no-one, apart from Thiery, knows that his aunty in Valence knew Chabal's mother from the launderette. No matter: Thiery's knowledge of French rugby is bound to be far superior to that of the ex-pats. But they begin to dither again, maintaining that a comprehensive grasp of one sport will not see them successfully through the quiz.

Christophe is resolute: 'Michel is a king amongst hunters – he knows everything about dogs and wild animals'.

'There is no hunting and very few dogs thanks to your brute', Michel reminds him; and Christophe concedes this might not have been his best suggestion of the evening. Then Bertrand, the quiet one, speaks:

'I have a telescope. I know about the stars'.

At this confession, a silence falls over the PMU bar like a shroud. Glasses are dropped in disbelief. People not involved in the discussion turn to stare in amazement. The smokers outside the open door stamp out their half used cigarettes and rush back inside just to be able to tell their future grandchildren they were present when THE ANNOUNCEMENT was made. Late night shoppers at the boulangerie abandon their evening baguettes and the word begins to spread. And somebody calls the pompiers.

'Et voila', exclaims Christophe. 'We have a team'.

As he pedals his bicycle unsteadily back down the road between Cabannes and Noves, Christophe, weaving in and out of the shadows, receives a garbled telephone call from Michel. Michel, if he ever had a first thought, has now had a second: he doesn't want to go to St. Remy. It's a step too far.

'Merde', says Christophe to himself. 'Where will I find the fourth team member?' And promptly falls into an irrigation ditch.

'Putain', says Christophe as he pulls himself and his weed-covered bicycle out of the irrigation ditch; 'no sense of adventure, these chaps' and looks round for his mobile phone on which, as he recalls, there is a useful light.

When Monsieur Villiers arrived back at the veterinary clinic in St. Remy in one piece, and bearing five jars of plum jam and a grin from one tiny ear to the other, he was greeted far more enthusiastically than he could have ever imagined. Knowing nothing of the (now referred to in capital letters) Battle of the Springer Spaniels, he thought it odd that the other vets, and especially Madame, the receptionist, should become so excited over one gift of confiture. However, he put their reaction down to that of rural types who don't see much action. When Monsieur Villiers explained that he would have to return chez Martin in a couple of days, the vets, having undertaken the briefest of formal discussions, asked him if there was the slightest possibility that he could stay for a month; just to provide injury — sorry, holiday cover. After all, they figured, a vet who was prepared and able to keep dangerous dogs away by overseeing home visits could only contribute to the much needed rebuilding of the clinic's reputation. Of course, they didn't explain it quite like that but it didn't matter: Monsieur Villiers said he'd be delighted, merci beaucoup. Thus began the secret, but entirely respectable, though emotionally charged, love affair between Madame Martin and the locum.

In order to keep the dangerous liaison above board, but simultaneously out of sight, and, of course, to retain his professional integrity, Monsieur Villiers has to devise a means of improving the health of Clovis. On the other hand, he doesn't want to be entirely successful or else there will be no justification for further visits chez Martin. It's a conundrum. Step by tiny step, he woos both Madame Martin and the dog; the second of these two now allowing him into its enclosure. And when he's not going in, Monsieur Villiers is taking Madame Martin out.

He really is quite the miracle worker. Clovis has stopped baying and snarling and Madame Martin, on an outing she particularly enjoyed, has been to Le Paradou to see the miniature village with all the tiny Provençal santons. It seems fortuitously easy for her to get in and out of her home unseen as, santon-like herself, she has no need to crouch down in Monsieur Villiers' car. And if Monsieur Martin has noticed the increasing number of times the veterinary locum drives up and down his lane, he's saying nothing. He's too busy himself, pretending to tend the small spotted ponies and irrigate his courgettes whilst secretly on a permanent lookout for tiny joggers in the direction of Noves.

Eventually, and as we could have guessed, le merde hits the fan in the kitchen. With one week left until the quiz night in St. Remy, and still with only three people in his team, Christophe arrives home from the mediathèque to enjoy a supper comprising fish pie. Madame Martin, on her way home from a visit to the santon maker in

Graveson, where, incidentally, Monsieur Villiers has bought her Daudet's wind-miller, has spotted the fish van in St. Remy and made a purchase and a pie.

Monsieur Martin looks up from his plate at Madame Martin. Christophe looks up from his plate at Madame Martin. Both see an unknown woman across the table; a woman with shiny hair, a clean face and a beaming smile.

'Where did the fish come from', demands Monsieur Martin?

Madame Martin stops beaming, having realised she may be in trouble.

'I took the bicycle to Cabannes', she replies, almost with a question in her voice.

Monsieur Martin, although not entirely convinced, lets the matter pass. But Christophe, who has recently harboured a number of suspicions about a number of things, none of which make any sense, suddenly has his eureka moment:

'Voila Maman', he cries. 'The answer is obvious'. Monsieur Martin looks up again, tired of his imbecilic offspring and the confusing supper. Madame Martin quakes:

'Comment?'

'Easy', says Christophe. 'Now you're able to get out and about, the problem is resolved'.

'Comment?' she shudders. Christophe can hardly contain himself:

'You, chère maman, will be the fourth member of the quiz team!'

Chapter Four

The assistant vet, previously confined in the physiotherapy department of the Henri Duffaut hospital in Avignon, has been transferred indefinitely to the psychotherapy unit, having been diagnosed with post-traumatic stress syndrome. Monsieur Martin has gone to Noves to see Dr Giraud with, as yet, undisclosed symptoms of who knows what. Christophe is in the enclosure with Clovis searching for clues to something also unknown, even to him. And Monsieur Villiers has taken Madame Martin on an outing to the Abbey of St. Michel at Frigolet where they are currently viewing the beautiful year-round crèche displayed just outside the gift shop.

The crèche, unlike those to be found at Christmas-time in the grand town halls of Avignon and Tarasçon, is not, it seems, dominated by the stable: over this crèche, Daudet's windmill towers supreme and the scenery is populated by all the characters found in his letters from that windmill alongside those from other Provençal folklore. Amongst these, in the foreground, is the Tarasque, now tamed and accompanied by St Martha. To their right, the boat she arrived on has just moored at St. Maries de la Mer where various Marys and Lazarus are disembarking. Jumping centuries and religions, the fat pope sits side-saddle on a stubborn donkey that refuses to move; whilst a peasant woman struggles down the hill, a huge bunch of asparagus under each arm.

Monsieur Villiers identifies several other characters and finally Madame Martin locates the stable and realises that the marching band, the bakers and the rice growers, the monks and the flower sellers, the three kings, who have arrived by horse, camel and elephant, and all the santons of the world are on their way to the nativity. For sure as eggs are eggs, Jesus was in Provence. Madame Martin is enchanted.

Afterwards, Monsieur Villiers and Madame Martin walk along the path, through a field where the wind is still rushing through the long grasses and up to the ridge of the Montagnette where, for the first time, Madame Martin looks down on Provence. On one side, she sees across the windswept plain to Tarasçon and Beaucaire, to Arles, to the Camargue and beyond to the place where she knows the sea laps at the shoreline. She looks behind and sees Avignon. She turns to the left and sees the Alpilles, the Luberon and, of course, the Ventoux which, like Daudet's windmill in the crèche, dominates the skyline. Madame Martin recognises another sense of her smallness in the world and thinks of Monsieur Martin and the little spotted ponies. When they get back, she tells herself, she will be kinder to him and to her son; except that, when they get back, Clovis has escaped.

Clovis has been feeling sorry for himself lately. In the old days, he muses, there was at least a frame of reference to a dog's life: you knew when food would arrive and you knew that when you heard the clink of glasses on the other side of the orchard, it was time to start barking. You knew that the third time someone shouted out of the window at you, it was time to stop barking. There was reason and structure; a point to it all. Then Monsieur Martin had arrived and taken him to St. Remy.

Before this unexpected event, Clovis had assumed that it was every dog's life to be tethered to a stump in a cage. He couldn't remember anything else. It had come as quite a shock to discover that dogs could be put on leads and made to sit in pick-up trucks. And it was, Clovis remembered, nothing short of amazing to find, in the car-park at St. Remy, that there were other smells to sniff. But when he got through the door of the vet's clinic and found all those stupid Springer Spaniels – well, it was no wonder that his world was in turmoil.

Just as Clovis was beginning to adjust to the fact that there might be something amiss with his existence, Madame Martin had, like some sort of Bernadette-of-Lourdes vision, mysteriously materialised from the rhubarb and begun filling his cage with tasty offerings. And if all of this wasn't sufficient to upset a dog's equilibrium, that funny little man from Marseilles had appeared in the enclosure, released Clovis from his tether and commenced to speak to him in forked tongues.

Through all these processes, each more disturbing than the previous, Clovis has tried as hard as a dog can to rationalise his life chez Martin. But when that imbecilic Christophe had come to poke around the cage this morning, just as Clovis had caught a whiff of a very interesting scent blowing across the orchard, and when the imbecilic Christophe had departed, leaving the cage door unlocked, Clovis has had just about enough of this constant and intrusive turn of events. He sniffs the air again and, relocating that exceptionally interesting smell, makes a break for it.

Chapter Five

Having, on occasion, referred to Phyllida's place, it should, before going any further, be made clear that Phyllida's place is not organised on a daily basis by Phyllida. Neither is it organised by Phyllida's partner who, being an intellectual, and possibly litigious in nature, remains not only nameless in this account, but will not be referred to any further than is absolutely essential to the narrative. It's true that Phyllida provides nutritional sustenance, invites guests and directs the aperitif, but only after consideration and priority have been designated to those who really run the place. These, in no particular order, are Lundi, Mardi, Mercredi and Jeudi: four extremely large cats of the Norwegian Blue variety.

At all times of the day and night, one must ensure that these joint lords of the manor are on whatever side of the door is appropriate to their continued health and well-being. Thus, after the aperitif, but before supper, Phyllida can be heard (virtually all across Provence) calling in her masters like a demented banshee: 'Lundi, Lundi, Lundi; Mardi, Mardi, Mardi; Mercredi, Mercredi – well, you get the gist; whilst the partner, whose name cannot be mentioned, raises his exasperated eyebrows along with his glass and turns up the volume of his latest Eastern European jazz record. Needless to say, the Norwegian Blues never respond to Phyllida's invitations, preferring to meander in as and when it suits them; leaving anyone present to debate whether, in the absence of dinner, another aperitif would be wise.

It is not, however, anywhere near time for dinner when Clovis begins to follow his nose across the orchard. In fact, lunch has only just been cleared away and Phyllida has gone down the road to see her neighbour, Louise, leaving the cats outside with the partner who cannot be named, but who, at just past two in the afternoon, is wondering whether it might still be a little early for the aperitif.

Being in the nature of an orchard, there are a considerable number of trees to circumnavigate. At first, Clovis does his utmost to mark out his newly found territory but, finding this tiresome, and tempted by the engaging smell he is currently following, he picks up speed and heads in the direction from which he has heard the clink of glasses each evening. The dog has accumulated a good turn of pace by the time he approaches Phyllida's hedge. Tail in the air, ears perked, nose wet and head held proudly high, Clovis is thoroughly enjoying his freedom when he is suddenly confronted by what seems to be an enormous mass of blue tinged fur with eight eyes. He stops in his tracks. Clovis, being taller than the little spotted ponies, is only familiar with small entities. Even Springer Spaniels are not large dogs.

' Can we help you?' The question appears to originate somewhere in the centre of the blue fur monster. Clovis takes a step backwards.

' Going so soon', asks the left end of the blue fur monster? Clovis, not wanting to appear impolite, is at a loss to know what to do. He can smell something different and suspects he is the source. Unfortunately, having never previously experienced fear, he is unaware that it has a tell-tale scent.

'Terribly sorry', he stutters, 'I seem to have taken a wrong turning'.

The blue fur monster makes a terrifying sound – somewhere between a cackle and a hiss – and leaps forward. Simultaneously, Clovis finds he is capable of a new noise, which will later be classified as a yelp, turns at right angles, and runs towards the far end of the orchard. On the other side of the hedge, the partner who cannot be named, and who has fallen into a temporary sun-blessed doze, is suddenly alerted to an unholy noise. He raises an arched eyebrow, pours the, largely melted ice, remainder of his post-lunch digestif down his throat, imagines he must have been dreaming, and promptly falls asleep again.

Meanwhile, over in Noves, Monsieur Martin has a terrible headache. He was not in possession of this headache this morning when he set off to see Dr Giraud. He didn't really have anything that you could put your medical, or otherwise, finger on; nothing further than a sense of anxiety and impending doom which, he felt, would be remedied by a visit to the doctor's surgery. In the event, the consultation has been a disaster; although, this observation remains unknown to Dr Giraud. The medical man has already forgotten the small, confused gentleman whom he met with an hour ago and for whom he prescribed the usual course of anti-depressants that every Frenchman and woman takes.

Monsieur Martin, however, now sat outside the bar-tabac nursing a small beer and a poorly head, has not forgotten what a mess he made of trying to find Sophy. He is awakened from his dismal thoughts by the urgent alarms of both the gendarmes and the pompiers who are screaming past, endangering the lives of anyone stupid enough to be pursuing their business outdoors in the afternoon.

'What's going on', Monsieur Martin asks an elderly lady who has just picked herself up from a heap on the pavement?

'Search me', she responds; 'une catastrophe on the road to Cabannes I believe'.

Down at the potato-packing plant, Christophe, who is just about to leave for a quiet afternoon at the mediathèque, has been called to the manager's office.

'There's a riot on the road to Cabannes', Christophe is informed. 'Collect as many men as you can. And bring ropes', the manager adds in the way that towels are unnecessarily called for at an unexpected birth.

At Mas Saint Antoine, where Phyllida has been visiting Louise, pandemonium has broken out and all the guests are locked securely behind the ornate iron gates with complimentary glasses of wine. Louise's normally placid lady dog, Nanette, who is currently in what is politely referred to as 'an interesting condition', has, according to some of the more hysterical guests, been afflicted by an onset of suspected rabies. Currently, she is running noisily up and down the inside of the ornate iron gates. On the other side, having finally shaken off the Norwegian Blues, and attained the origin of that very interesting smell, a wild dog sits in abject confusion, emitting his second new sound of the day. Clovis is crying.

Monsieur Villiers and Madame Martin, following all the sounds that are disturbing the normally peaceful road between Noves and Cabannes, have arrived at Mas Saint Antoine. Here they are greeted by the sight of pilots who are flying the water-gushing Canadairs overhead, the gendarmes, the pompiers, Monsieur Martin and a troupe of men from the bar-tabac at Noves, Christophe and a team of rope-bearing colleagues from the potato-packing centre, Phyllida, Louise, Louise's incarcerated guests, Nanette and, lastly, Clovis; in fact everyone, with the exception of the partner who cannot be named and who has just put on a new record by some obscure Eastern European jazz singer. All of the assembled turn to Monsieur Villiers and Madame Martin and greet them with the stony silence of accusation.

Chapter Six

There are so many unanswered questions, largely because, as yet, most of them have not been asked. And so many unresolved problems which no-one knew existed in the first place, that it's difficult for the gendarmes to know where to begin. They have no doubt that Monsieur Villiers and Madame Martin are the perpetrators because the crowd has obviously already reached this conclusion by the way they've made them the centre of attraction. In what crime these two might be the prime suspects is not so obvious, and is further confused by the large number of participants in the case being divided into two halves, either side of the ornate iron gates.

Nothing can be determined and no-one can be arrested, argue the gendarmes, until the two halves become one whole. That the one whole cannot be expected to form outside of the iron gates is clear. The half already thus placed has spilled onto the road between Noves and Cabannes causing tractors, trailers and cars to be backed up in both directions. It is rumoured that a television crew from Avignon are struggling to get through. If they are not allowed access, the people who live in Noves and Cabannes and on the road in between will not have their fifteen minutes of fame this evening and the national news will, yet again, be dominated by changes in the French rugby team.

In order for the two halves to become a whole on the inside of the ornate iron gates, something must first be done about two dogs who, to the astute gendarmes, seem to have played more than minor parts in whatever has occurred this afternoon. Accordingly, Louise is instructed to remove Nanette to a point on the estate where she can be tethered and remain unseen. The gendarmes then ask the owner of Clovis to step forward. Everyone in the half of the crowd outside the ornate iron gates takes a step back.

This causes those in possession of each of the front tractors in either direction to reverse into the vehicles behind. The drivers of the vehicles behind the tractors, and the drivers of the vehicles behind them, having also been shunted further back down the road, all leave their respective vehicles and begin to shout at each other, at the tractor drivers, and in particular, at the gendarmes. The gendarmes from Noves telephone the gendarmes at Cabannes to demand support in dealing with a major traffic incident. The gendarmes from Noves advise the gendarmes from Cabannes to attend on bicycles as there is no possibility of their car getting through this side of Christmas.

Monsieur Villiers, meanwhile, has walked over to the ornate iron gates, spoken to Clovis in forked tongues, and now has him secured on a rope that he has borrowed from one of the potato-packers. Monsieur Villiers offers to return Clovis chez Martin. A voice from the back of the crowd is heard to say, 'there's no way that bloody man's going chez moi on his own'. When the gendarmes are unable to locate the owner of this voice, Madame Martin says she will accompany the vet and the dog. Another voice in the crowd is heard to say, 'I wouldn't trust those two alone', but as the owner of that voice also refuses to be identified, the gendarmes agree that Monsieur Villiers, Madame Martin and Clovis should depart immediately. Further, they issue instructions that the last of this trio should be tethered somewhere out of sight, after which, the first two of this trio should return to Mas Saint Antoine tout de suite.

The pilots of the Canadairs, finding no reason to remain, radio the gendarmes from Noves to inform them that they are taking their yellow planes somewhere where they are needed but that, make no mistake, serious questions will be asked of the authorities if the person who suggested there was a fire in the first place is not apprehended. Let's be fair, calling the pompiers at the slightest turn of events is de rigeur but nobody messes with the Canadair pilots. As they withdraw, their position in the blue Provençal skies is immediately filled by the arrival of a helicopter, on board of which are numbers of journalists from Reuters.

Louise has tied Nanette to the central apex of a circular washing line. Phyllida has refilled the glasses of the existing guests at Mas Saint Antoine with more complimentary wine before going to the cellar in search of refreshments for those outside the ornate iron gates that are about to swell the ranks within. Meanwhile, down the lane that leads chez Martin, Monsieur Villiers and Madame Martin have returned Clovis to his enclosure. In this, they have saved a certain amount of time that they intended to pass looking for the hole in the fence through which Clovis escaped. They have saved this time by discovering that the door to the enclosure is open.

'Bizarre', says Madame Martin.

'Putain', says a voice from behind a tree trunk.

On their way back through the orchard, closely followed by a stealthy, unseen figure, they pass Phyllida's place.

'What's with all the helicopters', asks the partner who cannot be named? 'And why is Christophe stalking you?'

Madame Martin explains that she cannot explain; that she has no time being currently wanted by the police; but if the partner who cannot be named would like to join them at the neighbour's place, she is sure there will be an aperitif.

The partner, being an intellectual, possibly of a litigious nature and largely underwhelmed by the local gendarmerie, says 'merci' but he doesn't think he can be bothered right now. It will be too tiresome to round up the Norwegian Blues who have been missing in action all afternoon. Further, a new record by an unheard of Bulgarian jazz singer has just arrived courtesy of Phyllida's Amazon account. Moreover, he is already on his third aperitif.

'But do send my best wishes to Phyllida', he says, as if not expecting to see her before supper.

The major traffic incident on the road between Noves and Cabannes has almost been dispensed with. This is not so much due to the efficiency of the gendarmes from Cabannes as with the fact that, in the usual fashion, once the shouting subsides no-one is interested in exchanging insurance details. Back at Mas Saint Antoine, tables covered in pristine white linen cloths have been set under the fig trees. The two halves, now comprising a large whole, are, in true French spirit, combining their favourite national past-times: drinking the aperitif and talking.

'Merde', says Christophe to himself as he slips into the crowd, 'if only there was a competition in this, we'd be champions of the world'.

The cause and existence of the reported fire remains a complete mystery. Huge plumes of smoke were, indeed, seen in the orchard and none of the guests staying at Mas Saint Antoine are hesitant in taking ownership of calls to the pompiers; which, in turn, were relayed to the Canadair centre. The guests had, of course, been further distressed by an apparent outbreak of rabies that had been compounded by the arrival of a mad wolf outside the ornate iron gates. Nonetheless, there is no evidence to be found of a fire.

It's a mystery that might have been resolved had a certain person who cannot be named decided to forego the comforts of home which involve listening to an unheard of Eastern European jazz singer and not having to wait to be asked whether he'd like another aperitif. If the partner who cannot be named had joined the soiree at Mas Saint Antoine, he might have recounted how he was eventually woken from his siesta by unbearable noises emanating from an unexpected giant dust storm in the orchard that he had first thought was smoke. He might have further described how, on finally looking over the hedge, he had seen Lundi, Mardi, Mercredi and Jeudi, like a pack of lions on the Savannah, chasing a huge howling wolf round and round the orchard. He might have relayed this story, but he probably wouldn't have. After all, Phyllida was present and he was supposed to be in charge of the well-being of the Norwegian Blues.

Thus, as the evening progresses and the wine flows freely, it seems to the gendarmes that the case is clear. Which is to say, there is no case. There was no fire and there will be far too much paperwork if they start dealing with the foreign guests who called the pompiers, who called the Canadairs. Dogs will be dogs and those two have been separated and dealt with. No-one in the major traffic incident is pressing charges and everyone sitting at the tables under the fig trees appears to be happy. Well, everyone that is with the exception of anyone that has anything to do with chez Martin where there still remain a number of unanswered questions.

Chapter Seven

Finally, we can move ahead to the day of the quiz. Although now well into September, the evening is sufficiently balmy to allow those heading from chez Martin in the direction of St. Remy to travel not only inside, but also outside, the pick-up truck. Team PMU Cabannes comprises Christophe, Thiery and Bertrand on the outside, and Madame Martin, who is sat inside, on the bench seat next to Monsieur Martin. Behind them, in convoy, are Louise, Phyllida and the partner who cannot be named. They will be met at – to give it its proper name – Le Bar-Tabac des Alpilles by Monsieur Villiers.

In order to discover how this situation came about, it is necessary to go way back in time to a point before we ever met any of the characters in this account of life on the road between Noves and Cabannes. And, even though many of those who live in Noves and Cabannes might believe there's nothing much worth seeing of Provence, or of life in general, south of where they reside, and even though they are very probably correct in this view, there are, geographically, other places in the South before we reach those areas where the sea laps at the shoreline.

So, just as Monsieur Martin as a young man did, we must journey down to Marseilles; although we only have to do so in our minds and not, fortuitously, in the company of a troupe of performing poodles. Further, like Monsieur Martin, we have to acquire a little French philosophy; but nothing too challenging. Perhaps you've heard of laissez-faire? Perhaps you know what it means but, if not, picture a Frenchman giving a shrug of his shoulders. Voila: now you understand French philosophy.

When Monsieur Martin met the person who would become Madame Martin outside the big top in Marseilles all those years ago, she was a mere slip of a girl, much trampled upon by a family of acrobats. In fact, there were suggestions that she was not even related to those who stood upon her shoulders, being a foundling collected en route from the depths of the port. One thing, however, was clear to Monsieur Martin: here was a girl starved of affection. Never having had a friend of any description worth mentioning in these pages, a lonely insignificant woman, Monsieur Martin, a kindly man, not keen on baggage, immediately decided she was for him. He had long harboured a dream to own a smallholding where he could raise small spotted ponies and live from the fruits of the countryside of his birth in the company of une bonne femme.

We all know that life doesn't always fulfil its promises and Monsieur Martin has had his share of disappointments: he has an idiot for a son and heir; he has lost the friendship of Sophy; his herd of small spotted ponies has diminished; he has a mad wolf locked in a cage behind his home; and, until recently, he had a wife obsessed with confiture and daytime television.

On the other hand, he lives an undemanding life under Provençal skies in a place that the rich and famous have, thankfully, never heard of. He has neighbours who are equally as thrilled to live in this haven and who delight in the size of his courgettes. He has a son who, at least, has a job and now he has a dog that doesn't bark every evening. So, if he also has a wife who takes pleasure in the company of a veterinary locum well, so what, he philosophically shrugs: at least she's got her life back.

Naturally, there have, over the past few days, been threats, accusations, recriminations, confessions, explanations and, let's be fair, indecision and a complete lack of resolution. Nonetheless, the time has come to put this nonsense aside, at least temporarily. Compromises have been reached and now it's time to beat the ex-pats.

At the Bar-Tabac in St. Remy, Monsieur, le patron is brimming with joy at the arrival of Team PMU and assorted entourage, claiming never before to have heard of a French general knowledge team. (Reader, if you will, take a moment to consider this last description).

'These ex-pats', he continues, 'all very well and plenty of euro, but it's not the same as the old days'.

As St. Remy has been the centre of the ex-pat universe in France for so many years, to which particular old days Monsieur, le patron refers is unclear. He has a framed poster of last May's transhumance celebrations on the wall towards which he simultaneously nods and shrugs in a philosophical kind of way. Perhaps he means those old days when a few Provençal shepherds did the loop de loop round the town twice a year and everyone starved in between. It's irrelevant: tonight the place is packed with eight teams comprising English and Americans and one other team being the party from Cabannes.

'We've had to bow to the wishes of the majority', continues Monsieur, le patron, 'so the half time snack is English in origin'. Team PMU Cabannes and entourage give a well synchronised shudder.

'Meh bah', exclaims Christophe. 'Not burnt roast beef I hope'.

'Actually,' replies Monsieur, le patron, 'it's an unusual speciality – and very good too'.

Proceedings are directed by Madame Griffin, the multi-lingual directrice of the local language school who is married to an IT expert from New York, New York.

'We heard you the first time', says Thiery.

The first round is a picture round. Each team receives a sheet of ten photographs of people who they have to name.

'Putain', explodes Christophe, who hasn't recently viewed the pictorial archives in the mediathèque. 'What's this got to do with anything?'

'Don't worry', says Madame Martin, 'I've seen this lot in my magazines'.

'Don't worry', says Monsieur Villiers, 'I'll get another round in'.

In fact, all the teams at the Bar-Tabac in St. Remy appear to have a Monsieur Villiers type in their entourage who have been especially invited with the sole purpose of getting another round of drinks in.

The second round in the quiz is on English literature.

'Merde', says Team PMU Cabannes in unison, suddenly realising that a French general knowledge team does not mean the same as a quiz team in possession of French general knowledge. However, there are also mutterings from the teams representing the USA who, it seems, are under the impression that English literature means literature written in English and not by the English.

Round Three is 'name that tune'. Madame Griffin has forgotten to bring her special compilation CD so is reliant on Monsieur, le patron, to provide some tunes for the teams to name. As, with the exception of one track by Charles Aznavour, these consist entirely of songs by Johnny Halliday, Team PMU Cabannes begin to perk up. Having given up on the aperitif, and now sending their representatives for bottles of wine, the English and American teams are heard expressing their own unique translations of 'merde' and 'putain'. The partner, who cannot be named, is meanwhile busy making copious notes on the back of his bar bill.

The fourth and fifth rounds, respectively, concern themselves with world heritage sites and American politics. It's difficult to discern which team is the most distraught so this is an opportune moment, therefore, for Monsieur, le patron, to introduce the half time refreshments. These comprise bottles of Cotes de Ventoux, which everyone applauds, and tonight's speciality, Cheesy Chips O'Connor; named for a former illustrious customer who, one particularly raucous February evening, insisted on showing the 'chef' how to make 'proper food'. At the time, Monsieur, le patron, had been horrified but has since discovered that ensuring cheesy chips are on the menu during the winter months has more than compensated for any previous drop in seasonal income.

Team PMU Cabannes tot up the scores of the answers they believe are, thus far, correct. The partner, who cannot be named, for reasons already advanced, puts aside the book he has been reading on sixth century Buddhist philosophers, and transfers his notes onto a spare quiz sheet. He sits back with an air of indifference.

It takes longer than had originally been anticipated for either Monsieur, le patron, or Madame Griffin to organise the assembled into any sort of order appropriate to commencing the second half of the evening. Several people have demanded ice-cream which Monsieur, le patron, had not prepared for and for which he now tries, unsuccessfully, to make a charge. Most of the French contingent are outside enjoying a cigarette in the company of several Americans who, hitherto, have constantly maintained that giving up the weed was the best thing they could have done; apart from the rare occasion when they're in the company of the French. More wine is brought outside and for the first time in known official history, the French and the Americans begin to conspire against the Brits.

'Bloody ethnocentric', claims the IT expert from New York, New York and everyone agrees; although no-one can understand why a quiz run by a Frenchwoman and her American husband should favour the Brits. And no-one has any idea what, in English, French or American, ethnocentric might mean.

Eventually, tout le monde regroup for rounds six to ten. Round six concentrates on signs of the zodiac. Everyone in Team PMU Cabannes looks to Bertrand for the answers. Bertrand tries, quietly, to explain le difference between astronomy and astrology and everyone shouts at him. The following three rounds are foods of the world (excluding cheesy chips), famous animals (excluding Clovis) and French wines (at which everyone excels). The final round is anagrams. The Bar-Tabac at St Remy disrupts into chaos.

Finally, the answer sheets are submitted and more drinks are called for whilst some unknown person officiates. There is, as we might expect, a runaway winner. And, as we knew, even before the quiz began, the runaway winner is Team Who Cannot be Named. Chaos evolves into uproar. Uproar evolves into debate. Debate evolves into a general feeling of entente cordiale and bonhomie. And more wine is called for.

Part Two

Chapter Eight

For the last fifteen days, the mistral has rattled through the metal grids that house the bell in the church tower at Noves; has done its utmost to dislodge the stones that hold down the tiles on the roofs of Cabannes; has threatened the dried earth under which the new season's produce trembles fearfully; has screeched its destructive way through the dragon-infested nightmares of even those more resilient somnambulists. And has, it's alleged, been responsible for the arrival of at least one of the new patients in the psychotherapy unit of the Henri Duffaut hospital in Avignon.

This morning, however, those who reside in this wind tunnel have finally, as they knew they eventually would, woken to the clearest of blue skies in a world that is warmed by the glorious spring sunshine. Behind the road between Noves and Cabannes, Monsieur Martin and the partner who cannot be named are either side of a new wire fence that divides the place where the orchard used to be.

Monsieur Martin has temporarily abandoned his tractor and is busy tending his growing herd of small spotted ponies that have recently been freed from their mistral-proof enclosure behind chez Martin. Some are accompanied by their foals and all are greedily mowing the grass where old gnarled pear trees once stood. On his side of the wire, the partner who cannot be named is inspecting a young flourishing willow that was a gift from Monsieur Martin. It grows alongside a row of fig trees that the partner planted last autumn and which line, on one side, the new garden he has constructed in the place where other ancient gnarled pear trees once stood.

As well as the small spotted ponies, Monsieur Martin is accompanied by a dog that looks rather like a wolf and a person who, being no taller than the tallest of the small spotted ponies appears, to the unknowing eye, to be a pre-pubescent boy awaiting his growth spurt. The partner is accompanied by – in as much as cats ever accompany anyone – four large felines of the Norwegian Blue variety.

This crew once regarded the wolf on the other side of the wire as a cowardly intruder amongst the no-longer-standing ancient gnarled pear trees. And Clovis, for of course it is he, once perceived the Norwegian Blues as a fearful blue fur monster. But some things have changed.

It firstly falls on your narrator to account for the topographical differences in the environs and to this end we must turn to the demise of old Monsieur Règnier. It has not been necessary to refer to this gentleman earlier as, being intolerably old and infirm, according to his five sons, he had no active part in anything previously discussed. Moreover, the five sons – Jean-Pierre, Jean-Louis, Jean-Jacques, Jean-Ricard and Victor – have long since abandoned the simple life of Provence in favour of a more intricate existence in Paris. Old Monsieur Règnier did, however, play an indirect, unseen and marginal role in life on the road between Noves and Cabannes as he was the owner of the orchard between chez Martin and Phyllida's place.

Once a year, directing operations from his sick bed, Monsieur Règnier would issue a request to Thiery and Michel, via telephone to the PMU bar in Cabannes, to spray the fruit of the ancient gnarled pear trees for an agreed and agreeable fee. This was an act detested by both Monsieur Martin, who wanted to keep his courgettes ecologically and biologically sound, and by Phyllida and her partner who complained, quietly, of this annual arrival of poison floating over their hedge thus endangering the well-being of the Norwegian Blues.

At another point in the year, a second request would be issued from the sick bed chez Règnier which resulted in a troop of Eastern Europeans invading the orchard for two days of intensive picking and packing of the pears. This was not offensive to anyone (apart from the owner of the purse that paid them) and was, in fact, a welcome event for the partner who cannot be named as he could engage in conversation with the European picker-packers in order to update himself on current trends on the Bulgarian jazz scene.

To cut a laborious and arboreal story short, Monsieur Règnier has passed on to the great orchard in the sky and none of the sons want anything to do with pesticides, picking, packing or pears in general. They have agreed, therefore, that for a nominal sum, Monsieur Martin, Phyllida and Phyllida's partner can rent the orchard; and further, because the ancient gnarled pear trees were diseased and long past their prime, a description which they also use when talking of their father, they can be, as he was, removed. It goes without saying, of course, that no lawyers were involved in this arrangement. And because no lawyers were involved in this arrangement, everyone is trés content. Well, everyone apart from Madame Martin who was always quite keen on the odd jar of pear confiture.

Madame Martin is in her kitchen surrounded by three or four crates of speckled pears that she purloined during the final harvest, and which have been wrapped in straw during the winter months. They are, for a number of reasons, redundant in the jam department. However, mixed with chopped shallots, tomatoes and a number of secret ingredients, they will be perfect for a new variety of chutney that Madame has in mind. For jams and pickles containing secret ingredients, in their respective departments, are even more on Madame's mind than in earlier times; since when, she has also experienced some changes.

The most significant discovery that Madame Martin made last autumn was the existence and subsequent usefulness of l'internet. This she has mastered with the helpful tuition of Madame Lapin at the tiny mediathèque in Cabannes, to which she travels, by bicycle, three times a week. Madame Lapin, an aspiring feminist, who is naturally regarded with some derision down at the PMU bar, has become something of a friend and confidante to Madame Martin. They first met whilst browsing the confiture shelf at the local branch of Intermarché. Reaching for a jar of Reine Claudes, the librarian was unexpectedly tapped on the elbow by a small person she had previously overlooked. This, of course, was the diminutive lady from chez Martin who, with some bravado that must be acknowledged, proceeded to inform Madame Lapin that mass-produced, man-made Reine Claudes confiture was, not to put too finer point on it, merde. When Madame Lapin enquired about possible alternatives, Madame

Martin said she'd be only too happy to bring a jar of her own Reine Claudes down to the mediathèque and would lay good odds that, once tasted, the librarian and shop-bought Reine Claudes would never again be mentioned in the same breath.

At first, Madame Lapin, being an aspiring feminist, was horrified that, in this day and age, women were still shut in kitchens making jam and pickle, even if this was France. However, after only one spoonful of her green gift, she was won over and determined to help Madame Martin exploit her culinary talents. In order to give the jam producer the credibility and possible fame she deserves, Madame Lapin has been showing Madame Martin how to use l'internet to research old and abandoned Provençal jam and pickle recipes. Further, these two budding entrepreneurs are also investigating ways of establishing an online confiture business.

Of these developments, Monsieur Martin and Christophe are both ignorant. Similarly, they both claim to have no knowledge of the current whereabouts of Monsieur Villiers. The veterinary locum has not been seen or heard from since he suddenly disappeared just after Christmas, much to Madame Martin's apparent distress. We know that one of the new patients ensconced in the psychotherapy unit of the Henri Duffaut hospital in Avignon sits or, depending on the time of day, lies in the place once occupied by the assistant vet from St. Remy. The assistant vet from St. Remy, having been treated as far as possible for the post-traumatic stress syndrome he acquired following the visit of Clovis to the clinic, is now back at work. He is, naturally, limited in what he can do and spends his days with fish, lizards, small birds and pretty kittens not of the Norwegian Blue variety. It has been presumed, therefore, by anyone who's bothered to give the matter more than a passing nod, that Monsieur Villiers has returned to his original employment in Marseilles.

Nonetheless, certain people chez Martin have taken the locum vet's departure, without so much as an au revoir, ciao ciao, so long, farewell, or anything else in that line, as upsetting, rude, strange, disappointing and anything else in that line, depending on who's thinking about him. And frankly, whatever your perspective, it is rather odd. Apart from what he may or may not have felt or done for Madame Martin, the patience Monsieur Villiers displayed whilst working with Clovis during the time autumn gave itself up into the arms of winter was nothing if not miraculous.

Slowly, slowly, Monsieur Villiers won the confidence of both Clovis and Monsieur Martin and guided the pair into their current relationship. Let's be clear though, Clovis still lives in his securely locked enclosure behind chez Martin. If you, dear reader, have been harbouring hopes that this wolf-in-a-dog's-jacket has been sleeping peacefully on the hearth rug in front of a log fire, with a box of Belgian chocolates to paw, forget it! This is a story of country folk in Provence and has nothing to do with those ugly mutts that hang around in the handbags of Parisian ladies. But, with sound advice, Monsieur Martin took over from Monsieur Villiers and showed Clovis how much more pleasant life could be if the dog would like to stay off a rope and help with the small spotted ponies. So this wordless disappearance is très bizarre. Still, ponders Monsieur Martin, life must go on with or without Monsieur Villiers. There are more important things to worry about like courgettes, tomatoes and peppers. And, of course, the small spotted ponies, in regard of which, Monsieur Martin has a plan this spring which he also hopes will flower in the summer months ahead.

Chapter Nine

Let us return to that piece of land where the ancient gnarled pear trees once stood and that small pre-pubescent lad who we noticed earlier in the company of Clovis and Monsieur Martin. This is Gerard: not, of course, a pre-pubescent lad but a thirty-one year old man from the Camargue who, like several others in this story, stopped growing at an inopportune moment in time. Throughout his childhood and youth, Gerard had only ever aspired to be a Gardian like his father and brothers. To wear a brightly coloured shirt and nonchalantly sit astride a big white horse in the company of other Camarguaise, spending his days rounding up bulls and chasing them through the streets and across the river at St. Gilles was Gerard's one true ambition. Sadly, even though he'd passed all of his early summers preparing to fulfil his ambitions and knew everything about horses that there was to be known, including how to converse with them, the growth spurt for which he'd impatiently waited never arrived.

At last, when Gerard reached the age of nineteen, his father, glass in hand, took him to one side of the bar/tabac in St. Mairies de la Mer and gently explained that the son would never be a Gardian.

'I've got to think of the other lads', said the father. 'We'd get laughed off the face of the Camargue if we turned up at the parades with a midget in tow', he continued kindly. 'Think about another career. A plumber perhaps – they make good money for fitting into small spaces'.

So Gerard packed his tiny bags, kissed his tearful mother goodbye and set off on his travels. Anyway, that's enough about him; suffice to say that somehow, he has found his way down the lane from the road between Noves and Cabannes to where Monsieur Martin is delighted to have a genuine horse whisperer to help him in his new venture.

It's as if the so-called family unit down the lane that wanders away from the road between Noves and Cabannes comprises nothing more than a group of individuals, each proceeding with his or her own particular projects in their singular lives. In a way, as we know, this is nothing new: Monsieur Martin has been involved with the small spotted ponies for several years; Madame Martin has been occupied with jam jars since time immemorial; and, once he formally abandoned the education system at a non-prosecutable age, Christophe has packed potatoes and watched TV quiz shows. What's changed is this: whilst les Martins previously spent the time it took for their lives to pass by merely filling time and jars, at least two of the three now approach their days in a positive light with a sense of aspiration, ambition and purpose.

And not everything is detached, remote and singular for Monsieur and Madame also have a joint venture: Monsieur Martin is teaching Madame Martin how to drive. Monsieur Martin, whilst not wanting to be directly involved in the jam and pickle industry which has recently come to light, can see its potential. He can also see his wife's reliance on the feminist from the mediathèque. It's one thing for a wife to have a hobby and quite another to become vulnerable to ideologies and politics and general intimations of trouble ahead he thinks to himself. This type of nonsense demands more than a philosophical shrug of the shoulders. Monsieur Martin has concluded that the easiest way to remove Madame Lapin is to make her role as chauffeur redundant.

Cunning is not a trait generally associated with Monsieur Martin who, were he in possession of a shirt with sleeves, would display his heart and intentions thereupon. Therefore, he is happy to acquiesce to his wife's need for independent mobility by becoming her driving instructor. Madame Martin is also delighted at this unexpected turn of events, but not necessarily for the same reason. Ladies can also have a tendency to cunning if needs be. So, as the day's heat begins to dissipate, as the cicadas contemplate a slower tune, as sprinklers begin to whir in the orchards that remain on the other side of the road between Noves and Cabannes and as the glasses containing the aperitif emit a sociable clink in Phyllida's garden, Monsieur and Madame Martin clamber into the pick-up truck in preparation for the early evening lesson.

Naturally, they begin by driving up and down the lane until the resultant dust storm causes conditions and tempers to become unassailable. They then progress to Cabannes where, despite a noisy, but encouraging audience comprised of smokers and consumers of burgers and plastic pizza, Madame Martin practises a few manoeuvres in the car park opposite the PMU bar. After this, they move on to the much more challenging parking area at Intermarché. All of this is accomplished without major incident within the first week. Obviously, a couple of bicycles are written off along the way and Monsieur Martin is obliged to replace one fence post but, in general, all goes well. Each night, as they return and pass Phyllida's gate, those within raise a glass of cheer to empowerment.

Chapter Ten

Madame Martin and Madame Lapin, both armed with cameras and notebooks, have been up to a spot of industrial espionage at the local markets. They began innocently enough by simply observing the competition in the jam and pickle field but soon reached two conclusions: firstly, a successful online enterprise needs at least a hint of authenticity and expertise in order to tempt the target audience; and secondly, it may be preferable to initially establish a name locally. This brings a whole new meaning to the concept of knowing your market. And the main problem will clearly be how to gain the opportunity. Open air stalls they may be but breaking into this closed shop will be tricky. The same vendors have been selling the same goods on the same pitches to the same people forever.

St. Remy, for example, is currently a non-starter. A Mafiosi equivalent to that which controls the black diamond truffle trade over in the Var is in action here where plenty of euro are to be made from the Americans who will buy almost anything that smacks of foreign climes. Alternatively, the little market at Cabannes is also a lost cause owing to the fact that no-one further afield than Noves or St. Andiol has ever heard of the place. But, on this particular Friday, Madame Martin and Madame Lapin believe they may have found an opening.

Madame Lapin, along with her business partner, has made a right turn in St. Andiol, has passed the mural commemorating the local and national hero Jean Moulin. She has kept to the left over the difficult and dangerous junction, has passed through Mollèges without stopping for a pizza and has crossed the main road between St. Remy and Plan d'Orgon. Plan d'Orgon is a village where few venture and is signposted only so people know not to go in that direction. They have traversed the Route Jean Moulin which commemorates the local and national hero and, defying all attempts to thwart intentions, have secured a parking place in Eygalières. Well, let's just say Madame has abandoned her car.

For those that don't know, should you ever come into sufficient funds to purchase a property in Provence, a beautiful property in idyllic surroundings, where the little mountains of Les Alpilles watch safely over your villa that sits under the bluest of skies, surrounded by olive trees that produce the best oil in France; and where famous American movie stars compete with infamous French politicians for prime real estate governed by local legislation that forbids excess noise and thus pushes the famous American movie stars with their rowdy motor cycles and the infamous French politicians with their private-but-not-so-tasteful parties elsewhere; and where artists come from all over the world to paint the ancient but pristine chapel and wait breathlessly for a rare day when its doors might be opened; and where tourists climb the hill to swelter under the protection of the Madonna before descending for a crepe with Nutella and a glass of water; and where only the fabulously rich succeed in establishing a foothold alongside the locals in the place that is home to the local and national hero, Jean Moulin - well, this is where you'd be.

And if you lived here, you would, naturally, demand the exceptional produce that only Provence can offer: the best olive oil to drip on the greenest of green salads; the tastiest vegetables to grace your exquisite tableware that sits on the rough (but authentic) French linen; the finest wine to accompany the most succulent meat; the best lavender to scent your salubrious dining and bedrooms and, naturally, the best pickle to accompany your finest cheeses and the best jam to grace the surface of the freshest bread from the most perfect boulangerie. The Madames Lapin and Martin have a good feeling about today as they traverse the main and only street in the village surreptitiously snapping the odd photo for their scrapbook.

Monsieur Martin also has a good feeling about the day; although, to be fair, Monsieur Martin is an easily pleased man who has a good feeling about most days these days. His wife is out and about with renewed vigour and even though she is generally in the company of that feminist from the mediathèque, Monsieur Martin feels that the relationship is doomed: dependent solely on wheels it will, therefore, cease once Madame Martin is in possession of her very own driving license. And, of course, Monsieur Martin has neighbours that are so pleasant they have shared their limited funds and enabled him to own a paddock where once old gnarled pear trees stood.

Today, there are ten small spotted ponies in the new paddock: beautiful, calm creatures who are currently listening carefully to the ancient folk tales from the Camargue that Gerard is recounting. Gerard is sitting on a small stack of wood that is waiting to be transformed into a little hurdle for the small spotted ponies. If you were to wander down the lane that winds away from the road between Noves and Cabannes, along which you had lately been jogging, you would not be able to see Gerard and might pause awhile to consider the curious circle of interested and interesting small spotted ponies.

Monsieur Martin knows Gerard is a small but perfectly formed horse whisperer and he is eternally grateful for his miraculous appearance. Once the little hurdle has been constructed, and once the small spotted ponies have been instructed in its purpose, Monsieur Martin will finally be able to open his miniature riding school. All he needs is a vet to issue a health certificate; although that could be difficult since he is still banned from the veterinary clinic at St. Remy and Monsieur Villiers is still missing without a replacement. As Monsieur Martin ponders this bound-to-be insignificant problem, he suddenly experiences a sense of being watched. He looks behind towards chez lui and he also looks the other way down the lane. Nothing. Probably his imbecilic son he thinks to himself and, as on most of the rare occasions that he thinks of Christophe, he turns back and immediately begins to think of something else.

As it happens, this being a Friday morning, Christophe is packing potatoes. It's a tedious job but Christophe is so experienced that he can work quite efficiently without even thinking about it. This is quite a useful trait as Christophe has never been recognised for thinking about anything much in general. Obviously, there was a prolonged exception to this state of affairs last year when he spent a considerable amount of thinking time preparing for the quiz night at St. Remy. And a considerable amount of drinking time at the PMU bar trying to persuade others of their national duty to beat the ex-pats. Since that infamous evening there has been sporadic talk of a return match but no plans have ever been made. Last night, however, a few things happened that just might resurrect this embryonic idea.

The first thing that happened was that, as he entered the PMU bar in Cabannes for a small Pastis, Christophe noticed that it was served to him by a never-before-seen young woman. It's true she was so small that little of her body appeared above the bar. However, when she moved amongst the clientèle to collect the used glasses, Christophe could see that she was a perfectly formed being. Dark and swarthy, she was obviously from regions south of the South; which is to say, somewhere initially in the area of Marseilles but with a provenance that might suggest Italy or North Africa or another dark and swarthy clime such as Wales.

No-one else in the PMU bar has given the matter much thought and, very probably, neither would have Christophe if it wasn't for the second thing to happen. Christophe, watching the match on the big screen over the bar and minding his own business, which is no business, gives the dark and swarthy female a nod, a philosophical shrug and lifts his empty glass to indicate a refill is required. Antoinette – let's skip the formalities- arrives promptly to replenish the empty glass and to enquire whether she is serving the famous academic who initiated and coached Team PMU and inspired the legendary journey to the bar/tabac at St. Remy last year. Christophe falls in love.

Chapter Eleven

The two Madames continue down the main and really the only road in Eygalières. They pass the shop that sells the exquisite, but too well-hidden notebooks; they pass the stalls that sell the Provençal pottery. They pass the lane that leads down to tasteful boutique where Anais, with the help of her delightful daughter, Claudia, sells her even more tasteful clothes. They pass the cheese and the olives, and the vegetables that are spilling from their crates like runaway chickens. They pass Ganesh who, having married our dear Anais, sells his pristine white, Indian clothing. They pass the lady with all things designed to make a house smell welcoming and the woman opposite who has discovered the art of making curtains and tablecloths appear desirable. And they stop in front of a stall that sells confiture.

'No worries', says Madame Lapin. 'Look at it. Mutton dressed in a red checked scarf'. Things are looking good. They come to the end of the market but not the end of available space.

'This is it', they agree and look for the market inspector.

It's Saturday and Christophe has had a bath. A quick shower would normally suffice but Christophe, the academic wants to make sure that all the remains of the day, indeed of last week's existence, have been soaked thoroughly and have drained away down the plug hole of real life. Not a trace of potato, jam, dog, horse, earth, bicycle oil or any of the other combined scents (or sense) of a peripheral lifestyle are allowed to linger. Christophe is taking Netty, the barmaid formerly known as Antoinette, to dinner. Well, a pizza from the van in the square at Cabannes.

Christophe is astute enough to know not to talk about himself. Netty works in the bar and once word gets round that she has been seen out and about – sitting in the square – with Christophe, you can guarantee there will be no shortage of folk eager to update her in the life history department, including errant joggers. Meanwhile, Netty thinks that Christophe knows how to treat a lady: let's face it, he's given her free rein to talk about herself which, as it transpires, is quite interesting. Well, for these parts it is.

Netty is looking for her biological, biographical, missing father. Just as her new beau is keen on televised quiz shows, so the small dark beauty from the South is addicted to those 'find-me-a-family' programmes. She hasn't yet been lucky enough to have been selected as next week's star turn but she has completed a not inconsiderable amount of research. Basically, Netty believes that Papa stayed close to the port of Marseilles for many years but has latterly moved vaguely northwards; which is why, step by tiny step, she is migrating in a similar fashion. Christophe, ever the gentleman academic, thinks it's all a bit vague.

'Probably easier if you begin with his work', he suggests. 'Do you know what he does?'

'Alors', she replies, 'something with animals'. Christophe has finished his pizza, is in need of a beer and is also preoccupied with where he might take Netty next.

'We've got a small bloke from the South working with the horses at home', he offers helpfully. 'Come round tomorrow and meet him'.

There's not much that can be tastefully commented on regarding Plan d'Orgon. The trouble is that it falls just outside the eternally desirable triangle that comprises Avignon – which is where to go if you want festivals, opera and all things cultural, St. Remy – for ex-pats, Cheesy Chips O'Connor and expensive market stalls and Arles –

gateway to the white horses, flamingos and mosquitoes of the Camargue. We could go quickly through Plan d'Orgon on the Route Jean Moulin to see the statue of that famous local and national hero. Or we could stop at Plan d'Orgon if we wanted to see how the countryside can be destroyed by ravaging fires that were, allegedly, started by a local inhabitant and finally overcome by the Canadairs once they'd moved on from those iron gates outside Mas Saint Antoine on the road between Noves and Cabannes. Or we could, like most folk, just give it a miss.

Of course, this review is rather unfair to the inhabitants of Plan d'Orgon who, through no fault of their own, have to reside therein. Like everyone else in the South, they have lives to lead, thirsts to be quenched, stomachs to fill, crops to be harvested and animals to care for. There used to be a veterinary clinic in Plan d'Orgon but, until recently, they had no vet; largely because they had little with which to tempt a suitably qualified person. A few months ago however, after the fiasco at the clinic in St. Remy which had left a void in local livestock care, the mayor, under growing pressure from the locals, decided to allocate a small amount of taxes to re-opening this much needed facility. As there are few vacancies in the job market at Plan d'Orgon, a receptionist was soon found. And, surprisingly, the advertisement for a vet was answered almost immediately. The mayor wasn't too bothered about biography and references: the short dark man, clearly from south of the South, or somewhere dark and swarthy like Wales, obviously knew his stuff and was snapped up. So now there is a reason for folk who don't live in Plan d'Orgon to go there.

Monsieur Martin, still looking for a suitably qualified person to give the go-ahead for his miniature riding school, has recently learned there is a new man a few kilometres away. He called the telephone number he'd been given, left his name with the receptionist and is waiting for the vet to ring back to make an arrangement for a home visit. In fact, he's been waiting for three days and, as yet, he's heard nothing. Tonight, as the glasses clink pleasantly on the other side of the place where the orchard used to grow and where the guests are taking the aperitif in the new garden, Clovis begins to bark in accompaniment to the sounds of a recently delivered Bulgarian jazz record. As Monsieur Martin considers his plate of yet another fish pie, the same fish pie that reminds Christophe of unfinished business with the ex-pats, and while Madame Martin considers how much longer it will be before she obtains her driving license and subsequent independence, Monsieur Martin begins to mutter to himself.

It begins as a soliloquy on the inefficiency of veterinary receptionists, continues as a discourse regarding veterinary practitioners who are incapable of making an appointment, includes a philosophical consideration of how far throughout France news of Clovis and the Battle of the Springer Spaniels has travelled (even though the now baying Clovis is, allegedly, of improved character), is interspersed with subjective appraisal of the modern Bulgarian jazz scene and begins to conclude on the possibility (and expense) of a home visit. Except that Monsieur Martin fails to conclude because he is, somewhat surprisingly, given the usual lack of interactive dinner conversation, interrupted.

Firstly, Christophe, not a man known for opinions, wants to know more about the new vet in Plan d'Orgon. Apparently, Christophe knows someone from south of the South who is looking for a recent migrant who works with animals. Details are demanded and the news is broken that Netty will be visiting soon to meet Gerard. Monsieur Martin has no idea who Netty is, has even less of an idea why she would want to meet a rejected Camarguaise who tells ancient folk tales to horses, finds nothing in his imbecilic son's repertoire that relates to his own veterinary problems and, patient as he is, wishes Bulgaria will soon be destroyed by an unexpected shower of meteors. But what really confuses the mild mannered Monsieur Martin is the reaction of his generally silent wife.

Usually devoid of vocalised opinion, Madame launches into a barrage of vitriol: why does he need a vet and why can't he go to Avignon? Why does he want to go to Plan d'Orgon when no-one in their right mind goes to Plan d'Orgon unless they're on their way to see the monument to the famous local and national hero, Jean

Moulin? Why does he need a home visit? And why don't the bloody Bulgarians take music lessons? Monsieur Martin is somewhat taken aback.

Monsieur Martin delicately wipes a stray piece of baguette around his dinner plate and thereby gathers up the last of the sauce that has been holding the fish pie together. He considers eating the fish sauce-soaked bread but has little enthusiasm and quietly replaces his cutlery on his plate before silently leaving the table with a view to screaming at Clovis. The dog, however, is left to his own thoughts and Monsieur Martin wanders into the paddock to seek solace with the small spotted ponies. He notices the partner who cannot be named sitting alone with a large glass of something on the other side of the fence and they exchange Bonsoirs.

'Bloody Americans', says the man of a possibly litigious nature. 'The garden is full of them'.

Monsieur Martin, although having been sufficiently fortuitous thus far in life to have never experienced a group of Americans for the aperitif, perceives his own problems to be minimal in comparison with those of his neighbour and makes suitably soothing noises.

Chapter Twelve

The following Friday morning witnesses the Madames Martin and Lapin once again at the market in Eygalières. This week, however, they are not ambling down the main and only road of the village taking surreptitious snaps. Since une bonne heure, Madame Martin has been situated behind their own newly erected stall at the far end of the car park whilst Madame Lapin has been out and about freely distributing pickle and jam encrusted croutons amongst the crowds. There was some initial debate regarding who should carry out which of these jobs. The role of promoting the goods was deemed important until their location and produce became known and Madame Martin, being the more traditional in dress of the two, and not an aspiring feminist, had been considered the front runner. However, Madame Lapin, being the more forthright, and taller, was finally judged to be the better equipped, being less likely to be trampled upon.

The two women have done a deal with the prefecture whereby they have been allowed a temporary stall for two Fridays whilst their business registration is attended to in the chamber of commerce. Time, then, is tight: with only two opportunities to make their mark and warrant Madame Lapin's financial outlay, and Madame Martin's ensuing debt to her partner, it's vital that they do well today. Normally, as it's still relatively early in the year, this might have been seen as a risky business. However, the elements are with them: it's a gloriously sunny morning and the previously mistral-bitten locals are out in force. There is even evidence of a not insubstantial number of early tourists who are beginning to fly in from their winter resting climes. Despite some unpleasant spitting on the part of the other purveyor of confiture, that which is clothed in red checked gingham, it would appear that Madame Martin and her naked jam and pickle are making headway.

Meanwhile, in the paddock to the side of the lane that runs from the road between Noves and Cabannes, Monsieur Martin and Gerard have also made progress. During the past week, they have completed construction of the first of the hurdles and Gerard has begun to gently persuade each of the small spotted ponies to inspect the new edifice prior to considering a step over. The tiny Camarguaise is happy to give his full concentration to this most delicate of tasks because it stops him having to think about this evening's dinner. Gerard prefers to take his meals alone with his own thoughts but tonight his presence has been requested at the family table. Gerard is a self-absorbed young man who fears a break in routine. What he fears most though is the presence of an unknown female from south of the South who has also been invited to dinner with, inexplicably, the sole intention of meeting him. Gerard wonders whether he's expected to regale this person with folk tales from the Camargue. He can think of nothing else that he can possibly have to offer and his employer seems equally at a loss to elucidate.

In fact, Monsieur Martin is having trouble elucidating much this week: he has no idea whatsoever why the woman from south of the South is taking dinner chez lui. Monsieur Martin can't remember the last time anyone other than Sophy jogged their way to his dinner table. Actually, he reflects, looking over his shoulder for the third time this morning at nothing more than a vague feeling of being watched, no-one else has ever attended dinner in his house. Monsieur Martin briefly considers whether he should ask the partner who cannot be named for advice concerning the aperitif. This, however, might result in an influx of unknown Americans and the expectation of a Bulgarian musical interlude. And Monsieur Martin is also troubled by his wife. Again, this is nothing more than a nebulous concern, although he fears that money may have passed hands in the fast-moving events which have lead along the Route Jean Moulin this morning. And there's also the driving test which will take place tomorrow. Monsieur Martin wishes he had something more tangible to warrant his current feelings of uncertainty about life. Then he remembers that he still hasn't heard from the bloody vet at Plan d'Orgon and instantly feels much happier as this is a concern that he can do something about. 'Monday', he thinks to himself.

It's the end of the afternoon and Madame Martin has a lot on her plate, little of which is currently edible. The morning's work was far more successful than she and Madame Lapin could ever have imagined in their wildest dreams. Not that these two business women share much in the way of wild dreams. They already live in Provence which is the dream of most of the tourists who were seduced by their pickle and jam encrusted croutons so their particular approach to life is far more pragmatic. For a start, the earlier purchasing power evident in Eygalières has decimated Madame Martin's immediate stock of confiture and she faces a week of peeling, boiling and bottling in order to meet next Friday's demand. Before that can commence, however, she has to undertake and pass the long-awaited driving test tomorrow and amongst the wild dreams that Madame Martin hasn't experienced, is the expectation of passing the test first time. However, since arriving back home, she has learned that her husband, anxious to have his riding school certificated, intends to visit Plan d'Orgon on Monday to confront the errant vet. It is absolutely essential, Madame Martin reflects, that she does a left turn at the crossroads between St. Remy and Plan d'Orgon before her husband. In this, Madame Lapin, being one of the very few people in France who work on a Monday, will be absolutely useless.

Before these challenges, Madame Martin must provide a dinner of some reasonable description tonight for her husband, her son, the horse whisperer and an unknown being from south of the South or another dark and swarthy clime like Wales. Madame Martin contemplates a ratatouille whilst simultaneously coating a skinned and wine-drowned rabbit in swathes of mustard and wonders how her recently simple life became so complex. Her husband is currently filling all available space in the tiny fridge with rosé wine that he has discovered long buried in one of the outhouses. Christophe is, yet again, in the bath preparing for the soirée ahead. It's a quiet, but not very calming moment. The mobile telephone that nobody else in this household is aware of suddenly emits the buzzing vibration that notifies Madame Martin of an incoming text message. She reads it, turns it off and hurriedly replaces this newly discovered means of communication back in her apron pocket.

By 8 o clock, all those expected for dinner have arrived and Monsieur Martin is very pleased with the outcome of the aperitif which commenced an hour previously. It's true things were a little stilted at the beginning of the evening but our host has decided to follow the example set by those on the other side of the place where the orchard used to be and make a meal of the aperitif – in a manner of speaking. In this, he has chosen the best of the traits offered by his neighbours; which is to say that no Bulgarian jazz records or music of any description has been involved. On the other hand, glasses have been topped up far more frequently than might normally be the custom which, in turn, means that tongues are far looser than might generally be the custom.

Christophe's friend, Netty, has been welcomed with all the politeness that the French can muster - which is a great deal in comparison with the efforts of some other nationalities – before being expected to make her own way through the evening's labyrinth. As Netty is French, although possibly of a darker and swarthier provenance, this presents no problem. For the last twenty minutes she has been questioning the quivering Gerard with a determination that has matched Madame Martin's attempts to worry the mustard-covered rabbit into the oven and construct the accompanying ratatouille whilst re-reading her highway code and maintaining the impression that all is well. And as Madame Martin, Monsieur Martin, Christophe, Netty, Gerard and the rabbit are all much the same in size, and all are equally soaked in wine, they feel that the event is not looking too demanding after all.

As this troupe troop to the table, Netty surmises that, in one respect, her quest has been unfulfilling: Gerard may well originate south of the South but because he is, depending on where you're facing, from west of the south of the South, in a place where it's hard for those who are from east of the south of the South to break into, he knows nothing of the whereabouts of her missing father.

Conversely, he has been able to inform her, from second-hand knowledge garnered from his frustrated employer, that someone directly from the south of the South is currently a veterinary practitioner in Plan d'Orgon. This is news which is potentially more promising although Netty is at a loss to understand why it provokes such a tirade of abuse from Monsieur Martin and such an obvious display of concern from Madame Martin. When Christophe, fed up with all the attention that the horse whisperer has been receiving from his beloved, offers to take Netty to Plan d'Orgon on Sunday, Monsieur Martin informs him that he can join the bloody queue of people seeking this modern day Scarlett Pimpernel. Madame Martin promptly bursts into tears. At this point, there could have been a very unpleasant turn of events but, as often happens in life and literature, there is an unexpected knock at the door. Clovis whines.

Chapter Thirteen

Madame Martin, surrounded by a number of small spotted ponies, sits on the newly constructed wooden hurdle in the paddock disconsolately spooning blackberry and apple confiture into her tiny downcast mouth. It is Sunday and the small spotted ponies, who hate Sundays because it is Gerard's day off, are hoping for an interesting folk tale from this unexpected interloper. Madame Martin has stories of Provençal life that they wouldn't believe; true stories that would make the small spotted ponies whinny in distress; stories that would make them canter away in contempt. Madame Martin, however, remains silent. She has no memory of where her story commenced and even less of an idea where it might finish. The only certainty is that she is alone: Christophe, Netty, Monsieur Martin, Gerard and Clovis have all left in the pick-up truck, via the Route Jean Moulin, to Plan d'Orgon. For various reasons, they have all gone to confront Monsieur Villiers. Of course, the only person who knows the elusive vet's identity is the only person who hasn't gone on this excursion.

And, at the risk of rhetorical questioning, where, dear reader, should your narrator begin with that which, as yet, is unanswered? Did Madame Martin pass her driving test yesterday? Well, the answer is 'yes'; but, in the short term, this fabulous accomplishment is somewhat redundant as any inclination she had to speed over to Plan d'Orgon to warn Monsieur Villiers of an impending visitation by almost everyone she knows, with the exception of Madame Lapin who knows nothing, has been thwarted by the commandeering of the family vehicle by almost everyone she knows, all headed in a similar direction; apart from Madame Lapin whose whereabouts, this weekend, are unknown.

Why is Monsieur Villiers practising his veterinary skills in Plan d'Orgon where people seldom venture unless they are en route to see the memorial to the local and national hero, Jean Moulin? Well, on a superficial level, for the same reason that mad people climb

Everest; which is by no means on a superficial level. It was a job. Of course, anyone who has read the initial accounts of life along the lane that runs off the road between Noves and Cabannes, anyone who has the slightest understanding of human relationships, particularly those conducted in the South, will know that all the bonhomie exhibited at the bar/tabac in St. Remy on the infamous quiz night, and that which followed, is a mere fabrication of true life in France. One only has to look at one's politicians for exemplars. Of course Monsieur Martin retained an unabated suspicion of the intentions of the vet. And obviously Christophe, overcome at last with a sense of his own self-worth on the night, continued to hate Monsieur Villiers with a purpose matched only by his desire to form a worthwhile quiz team for the return grudge match. And naturally, dear reader, Madame Martin and Monsieur Villiers remained cocooned in their mutual affection.

Who had come knock-knocking at the door of chez Martin at such a timely moment the other night? To all intents and purposes it was Phyllida armed with a selection of Bulgarian and Romanian jazz records. It seems that the partner who cannot be named, aware that a rare soirée was in progress on the other side of the place where old gnarled pear trees once grew, was consumed by anxiety for his willow-giving friend's skills as a host. Unable to hear anything other than the whine emitted by Clovis, the partner felt that a musical contribution was needed to create a suitable mood of well-being. He had, therefore, instructed Phyllida to deliver a carefully chosen selection of the jazz that he deemed essential to the construction of une bonne ambience.

The records had been received with a certain degree of over-the-top gratitude and Phyllida, declining the somewhat half-hearted offer of a glass of rosé, had been politely dispatched back down the lane to her own side of the fence. Although, as Madame Martin now recalled, there was something slightly odd about the episode. On opening the door, she had discovered Phyllida looking over her shoulder as if she had suddenly found herself jumping a no-longer existent queue of callers. Madame Martin also looked over the shoulder that Phyllida was looking over and felt certain that there might have been someone else in close proximity. However, no-one else was jogging their tiny way back down the lane towards the road between Noves and Cabannes and she could see nobody hiding behind the lavender bushes. The notion was dismissed along with the neighbour.

Madame Martin wonders, as most women at some time or other do, how she could have been so foolish. Compared with her situation a mere two years ago, life has undergone a transformation beyond any of the wildest dreams that she has never entertained: she now has, as every woman needs, a female friend, mentor, business partner and partial confidante in Madame Lapin. With the help of the latter – one might say at the instigation of the aspiring feminist – Madame Martin has the wherewithal to produce delicious jam and pickle from old Provençal recipes to much acclaim; so much so that a promising future is quickly emerging from its embryonic stages. She has passed her driving test and has all the independence that this brings to look forward to. Her husband is on the way to success with his miniature riding school and Christophe – here Madame Martin falters, but that's always been a difficult topic even if he is her only son and heir. However, like many women before her, and legions yet to arrive, Madame Martin confused her priorities by falling in love. She looks at the rogue mobile telephone for the umpteenth time to see whether a new message has secreted its way into her apron pocket. Nothing.

Nearly four hours have passed since the pick-up truck made its way down the lane towards the road that runs between Noves and Cabannes. The ever practical Madame Martin has long since left her ruminations behind in the paddock and returned to the kitchen to commence preparations for a new stock of goods for this Friday's market in Eygalières. Finally, she hears the vehicle arriving home and the unexpected sounds of a happily chatting entourage as they spill into her jam-covered environment. She looks warily at her husband:

'Did you find the vet', she asks? Dangerously.

'What? Oh no', Monsieur Martin replies. 'The place was shut. It's Sunday', he explains joyfully.

'Well, where have you been all this time then', inquires the daring inquisitor?

'We've been to see the memorial to the famous local and national hero, Jean Moulin', comes the enthusiastic response. 'C'est fantastique!'

Despite the successful Sunday outing which resulted in the French contingent finally viewing a part of their history, the initial reason for the trip to Plan d'Orgon is not forgotten. On Tuesday morning, Monday having been discarded as a time when anyone in La France, apart from Madame Lapin, might be gainfully employed, Monsieur Martin telephones the vet. However, having had twenty-four thoughtful hours in which to make important business decisions, Monsieur Martin, much to his frazzled wife's relief, has decided he's had enough of Plan d'Orgon and has contacted a veterinary practice in Chateurenard. There might well be a vet in Plan d'Orgon, he thinks but, on the other hand, it may be nothing more than a vicious rumour. And in any case, business is business – or will be if the miniature riding school is ever up and jumping – and too much time has been expended waiting for replies, arrangements and visits that never happen. In this, Monsieur Martin has taken counsel from the partner who cannot be named but who once had a job; the gist of which also cannot be accounted for but which obviously involved some hard-headed resolutions.

Of course, the partner is of a litigious nature that is as far removed from Monsieur Martin's outlook on life as the philosophy of the seventh century Buddhist monk which informs the neighbour who resides on the other side of the fence: not for him any of this nonsense. Nonetheless, the man who lives with Phyllida, if we may safely accord him such provenance without fear of legal recourse, shares a love of animals, courgettes, tomatoes and wine, as well as a suspicion of Americans and is, therefore, deemed some sort of authority in the advice-giving field. And his advice was, 'go elsewhere'.

Monsieur Martin had not previously thought of looking in Chateaurenard being, as it is, a concrete island in Provence concerned mainly with the transportation of anything to all areas of France. Which is to say, initially involving itself with the distribution of Provençal market garden produce to almost anywhere, it has evolved into a gigantic lorry park which anyone with any sense rushes through just for the safety of being somewhere else. However, and against all expectations, a vet has not only been identified, but will call chez Martin tomorrow armed with reams of the appropriate paperwork necessary to round up and move on the small spotted ponies like some bureaucratic stampede.

In the meantime, Christophe, whilst physically exhausted by the unexpected five mile trip to the memorial to the local and national hero, Jean Moulin, has been dutifully inspired by this discovery of his heritage. Here, virtually on his doorstep, is a whole new area of research with which to attack the ex-pats at the grudge match which he is now even more determined to organise. This Jean Moulin fellow, he has ascertained, played a significant role in supporting the allies in the Second World War. That would be the British and American allies, the descendants of whom now inhabit the locale and who should jolly well know better. It's potentially shared knowledge and thus justifiable for a round in the quiz that he's determined will take place in the PMU bar in Cabannes.

In this, Christophe has his own ally, although not one of ex-pat origin unless you can count the possibility of a Welsh influence. Which he doesn't. Netty is keen to find Papa but, at the moment, she is keener to hang on to Christophe, the academic and is fully supportive of his increased elevation in Provençal affairs through the suppression of the ex-pats in a return match. Being of good character, and not unattractive, she has influence over the proprietor of the

PMU bar in Cabannes and has already begun to weave her assertive and persuasive magic in regard to the much anticipated home game.

For Madame Martin, then, it's a time to draw breath; a time to peel and boil and bottle; a time to build up marketable resources; a time to wait for news from the Chamber of Commerce; and a time for further furtive vibrations from that which is hidden in her apron pocket.

Part Three

Chapter Fourteen

There's something amiss with Madame Lapin. Madame Martin finds it difficult to place any of her tiny fingers on the source of her disquiet but, with a woman's instinct about other women, she knows it to be a Provençal truth. For a start, the aspiring feminist, who previously couldn't give two hoots about her appearance, has begun to lose weight. Madame Lapin has also given up on all those baggy sweatshirts and shapeless trousers and now sports a more tailored appearance. She's not only taken to styling her hair, but has obviously made surreptitious visits to the coiffeur to have something done with her roots. Moreover, this is clearly not the coiffeur in Cabannes but somewhere further afield: somewhere with more up-to-date magazines perhaps. If we didn't know better, we might think that Madame Lapin is trying to impress someone.

Madame Martin is perplexed by her preoccupation with Madame Lapin that she can't seem to shake. To all important intents and purposes, their relationship is progressing well: their now permanently established stall in Eygalières is one of the most popular on the market. Locals and tourists flock to purchase their jam and pickles and the competitor with the gingham dressed jars has long since departed in a fit of weeping and spitting. The Madames are about to try out a second stall on Sunday mornings in Isle sur la Sorgue. This is a clever move: the place is crawling with American tourists, even wealthier than those in St Remy. Further, the ladies have found Gaston, a hapless youth in Cabannes who, despite having little else to add to his potential portfolio of life skills, knows how to design a jam encrusted website in his tiny back bedroom. The online business is a mere click away. So what is Madame Martin's problem?

Despite acquiring her own driving license, the diminutive lady who resides down the lane that runs from the road between Noves and Cabannes still travels in the company of the taller lady from the mediathèque. To share the ever increasing costs of fuel, they sometimes go in the Martin pick-up and other times á la Lapin. They rarely journey alone. Well, not to each other's knowledge at least. One of them may well take the odd sortie in the direction of Plan d'Orgon with no intention of visiting the memorial to the local and national hero, Jean Moulin, but at no disruption to business. Business is business and plans are plans. Although some plans may not coincide and some business might be no-one else's business. For example, some of Madame Martin's plans have nothing to do with her partner. Further, despite all those 'instincts', she has mistakenly assumed that Madame Lapin has no business that doesn't concern the two of them. Madame Martin, therefore, cannot understand this notion of a gulf she sometimes feels.

Of course, it's not simply a matter of unexplained metaphorical distance that concerns Madame Martin: there's also the geographical expanse of a ten mile round trip to Plan d'Orgon to negotiate in weeks which are packed from one Friday to the next with peeling, boiling and bottling. Whenever it occurs to Madame Martin to confide in Madame Lapin, she soon pushes this potentially dangerous notion back into the darkest recesses of the jam jar store; in these pickle-filled days, there are few beans of interest to spill. In any case, although Madame Lapin's inability to make jam and pickle is a little irritating, Madame Martin knows that her business partner's spare time is equally occupied with supervising Gaston in the design of the website and organising all the online administration. Madame Martin could really do with one or two people to help her in the kitchen.

On the other hand, Monsieur Martin, having little to worry him in the department of personal issues, and recognising his priorities, has now successfully established the miniature riding school. He plans to hold an official opening later in the summer, hopefully to coincide with the annual village fête. However, he already has half a dozen children from Cabannes who arrive every Saturday morning eager to ride and jump their way around the paddock under the gentle instruction of Gerard. Watching from the other side of the fence is the partner who cannot be named, but who very much enjoys this new weekend spectacle.

The partner's patch is literally blooming. It's almost unbelievable to think that this time last year the scorched earth was packed tight with old gnarled and diseased pear trees. You might have thought that, with the best will in the world and untold optimism, this was no place for a pleasure garden. However, the partner's philosophy is not guided by notions of best will or optimism: he is led by a combination of the advice of a 7th century Buddhist priest and the long term effects of a regime entirely dependent on an early aperitif. Slowly, slowly does it for him.

Behind the back of the converted garage that he shares with Phyllida, the partner already has a well-established garden of a different variety. This earlier creation reflects the intensity of the landscaper's personality, being a virtual rainforest of darkness which must be watered three times daily during the height of summer. Irrigation, for the benefit of those who dare to undertake such responsibility during rare moments of the partner's absence, is helped by the location of strategically placed colour-coded signs within the spider-infested jungle. One must always fight through the undergrowth to begin the procedure at the end. Walking backwards, the water-bearer then tends the various varieties of bamboo, the lush leaves of the fig trees, the pale pink showers of tamarisk, the smaller prehistoric plants and so on. Eventually, one regains a foothold near the gate in a state of oppressive claustrophobia and paranoia. Even the cicadas shy away. Apart from the partner who cannot be named, there are only four beings that enjoy this terrible environment: they are blue and from Norway.

In comparison, and coming as something of a shock to Phyllida, the new garden reflects a man she has yet to meet. It is light and airy and the cicadas and butterflies have colonised a new and welcome home. A wealth of multi-coloured flowers, although precisely planted, gives the impression of a randomly floating magic carpet. Water, running down a feature made from reclaimed material, trickles more musically than any Bulgarian input in this multi-sensory garden. Tiny birds sit in the shade of the little trees that have been planted along part of the wire fence that divides the land from that of Monsieur

Martin. The man of a possibly litigious nature had fully intended to cut himself off visually from goings-on on the other side of the fence by planting even more trees. However, as he reclines upon his self-made wooden chaise-lounge, glass in hand, watching the small spotted ponies jumping the even smaller hurdles, he has changed his mind.

Phyllida, meanwhile, having abandoned an earlier vegetable garden due to a previous overload of spare courgettes and tomatoes from the semi-naked and often passing Monsieur Martin, has now started work on a new fruit and vegetable patch. The loyal Monsieur Martin still stops at her gate with the odd gift but, since Madame Martin's jam and pickle business took off, every spare potential ingredient that originates chez Martin is snapped up and thrown into the boiling pan before there's a chance of it making its way down the lane. Phyllida and the partner who cannot be named are vegetarians so fresh supplies need to be more regular in appearance.

And Madame Martin, with the help of her husband, has also taken up the gardening craze. It seems a lifetime since she took those first tentative steps through the kitchen door and fought her solitary way through the brambles and rhubarb to the enclosure in which the unhappy Clovis spent his lonely days. Now, however, with an increasing need to source produce to make her jams, this same area has been carefully planted with raspberries and blackberries and other assorted fruits, all neatly harnessed within a maze of bamboo canes.

In an area of Provence long known for its horticulture, it's good to see the sun beating down on all these keen gardeners. Over at Mas Saint Antoine, Louise has removed all the expensively purchased, mosquito-repelling but evil smelling bushes that interfered with the pleasure-taking clients in the pool. She has replaced them with lavender that is worshipped by the bees and hummingbird hawk moths. Mosquitoes are rare in these parts and if they do return, Louise has decided that it will be preferable to ply her guests with copious quantities of rosé rather than have them screw up their noses under the suspicion that the Norwegian Blues have gained entry and left their mark. Her husband, meanwhile, spends his days roaming the parkland aboard this year's model lawn mower from which he views his neighbours' attempts to improve the adjacent landscape with some satisfaction. Let's face it, business is also business at this juncture on the road between Noves and Cabannes and online table d'hôte ratings cannot be allowed to decline.

With one exception, then, everyone is busy exploiting the delights of Provençal nature. The only person not involved in the gardening rush is, of course, Christophe but that's only what we would expect from an academic. Christophe is busy trying to nurture his beloved Netty and simultaneously organise the return grudge match between Team PMU and the ex-pats who pass their retirement in the bar/tabac over at St Remy. He's finding it tricky to prioritise or even juggle these responsibilities: experience shows it's difficult enough to locate an attractive young lady in these parts, let alone stop her from jogging off into the sunset over at Noves. On the other hand, Christophe has a reputation of other sorts to maintain: he's a scholar; an event organiser; a Frenchman with a determination to overcome international opposition. He's also a potato packer with a girlfriend intent on finding a father from south of the South. It's all becoming too confusing but, because he knows he has a duty to prevail in the field of citizenship, Christophe has created further potential problems for himself by joining the annual fête committee.

Chapter Fifteen

Clovis is bored. It's been a long time since he saw action of any description. Certain actions involving nasty shocks he could well do without, but there are other vague memories that he nurtures: the battle with the Springer Spaniels is one of his favourites. The visit to Mas Saint Antoine to see the delicious Nanette is another. Clovis feels life is a little unfair: it's true he spends his days with Monsieur Martin or Gerard in the company of the small spotted ponies which, of course, is far preferable to being shut in a cage behind the house. However, Clovis sees this quasi-freedom as payment in kind for his generally good behaviour; quid pro quo he might maintain were he proficient in Latin like the man on the other side of the fence. Clovis, however, is not particularly proficient in anything. He, does, nonetheless, have a notion of injustice plus a nagging sense that both of his favourite memories smack of unfinished business. The small spotted ponies are busy partaking of a hay-break, so Clovis wanders over to the fence that separates his territory from that of the blue-furred monster. The Norwegians are nowhere to be seen but the partner who cannot be named is relaxing on his wooden chaise-lounge.

'Bonjour Clovis', says the partner. 'You look bored'.

Madame Martin is driving to Noves along the road from Cabannes where she has just finished a business meeting with Madame Lapin. The once aspiring feminist was wearing a pair of leopard-skin print leggings, a rather low-cut black silk blouse and precariously high-heeled shiny shoes. Madame Martin was wearing a fruit-splattered apron and a discarded pair of Monsieur Martin's gardening boots.

Madame Martin, who was obliged to view Gaston's updated website in the back bedroom, wondered whether Madame Lapin was going somewhere else afterwards. She failed to pursue this thought, however, having more important matters to discuss: the problem is, she informed her business partner, the move to Isle sur la Sorgue would have to be deferred indefinitely unless or until they could afford to employ someone to help with the jam and pickle making. They simply didn't have sufficient supplies or time. Madame Martin was sieved and drained of all energy in case her partner hadn't noticed. Madame Lapin had crossed her animal clad legs, considered the matter and concurred that this unseen expense was, unfortunately, necessary. So now Madame Martin is on her way to Noves to fill the employment void. Except that there is no need to travel all the way to the next village for here, jogging along the road, just outside Mas Saint Antoine, is a likely candidate.

Those with a sound memory, of whom there are few locally, will remember that Monsieur Martin had a paternal penchant for Sophy. This was precisely because she had no desire to spend her Provençal days indoors, preferring to be outside with the small spotted ponies. However, that was in the strange time we call 'the past'. These days, the novelty of Dr Giraud's personal therapies, as we might have suspected, has worn a little thin. It's not that Sophy is necessarily desirous of Christophe's company; it's just that she's heard that someone else might be in the frame. And she misses Monsieur Martin whose success with the miniature riding school she would very much like to be a part of. When Madame Martin asks whether she might be interested in a few paid hours helping in the kitchen, Sophy shudders inwardly; then, perceiving this as a way back into all sorts of folds, she agrees to the minimal terms and conditions.

Madame Martin wonders whether she has time for a wash, a change of clothes and a quick trip to Plan d'Orgon. It all seems too exhausting and not for the first time, she wishes she could join those continual parties for the aperitif over at Phyllida's place. Madame Martin employs the twenty-three point turn and in so doing, notices another sorry looking female: Nanette, wearing an expression of deep sadness, has her head stuck between the bars of the ornate iron gate of Mas Saint Antoine. A number of guests, disturbed from their pool-side relaxation, have arrived with helpful suggestions in a variety of languages. In the background, Madame Martin sees Louise's husband parking the lawn-mower with a degree of resignation. In the foreground, his wife has arrived with two bottles of rosé wine. Madame Martin drives home.

Chapter Sixteen

Christophe has attended another fête committee meeting in a room above the PMU bar in Cabannes. Christophe's quiz team meetings previously took place in a rowdy corner downstairs so he has been somewhat in awe of the secluded officialdom of these superficially more organised events. However, he soon realises that, hitherto, there has been little to discuss. He acquired his place on the committee by virtue of the fact that someone noticed that someone else had died. According to the rules of the commune, there must be a quorum of six in order that meetings can be registered. The other five comprise founding fathers that have run the annual village fête since time immemorial. In the interests of time management, they have largely followed the order of play previously designated. Change and Cabannes are seldom recognised as appearing in the same sentence.

Thus far, the only problem presenting this year is who will provide the paella. Henri, who has performed this duty admirably for the last twenty-five years, is, they all agree, on his last legs. In fact, at this very moment, Henri is in a heap on the floor of the bar below. Jean-Pierre Lucard from Orange is now the front runner. It's some distance for Jean-Pierre to travel but the price is right and he's oh–so–popular. Appearing as he always does, on his shiny silver trike, his pale blue shirt vaguely unbuttoned to show both his golden neck chain and a suggestion of promise, men proudly view him as the epitome of a macho Frenchman. Naturally, the ladies see Jean-Pierre Lucard in a similar light but they have slightly different ambitions in the departments of anticipation, hope and satisfaction. No matter, Jean-Pierre will pull the crowds one way or another. Christophe has no interest and will not raise an objection. In fact, Christophe will not raise an objection to anything. He wants the waters to be calm when he introduces his idea for a quiz hosted by the village.

Monsieur Martin, having previously submitted six copies of a written request to present his suggestion that the small spotted ponies be allowed to join the parade, is also in attendance as guest extraordinaire. The main business has been completed in record time. There is official agreement to finance the services of Jean-Pierre Lucard, and the Pastis glasses having been refreshed, the committee sit back as Christophe takes centre stage. Of course, Christophe could just go ahead and organise the quiz independently. However, he is wise enough to realise that the grudge match will acquire far greater kudos if it becomes an integrated part of the annual fête. Committees are committees; which is to say that, in this neck of the woods, anything bearing the official stamp of a recognised quorum of elders is seen to comprise a necessary element of democracy. That crowd over at St Remy could hardly turn down an invitation to Cabannes for a return match which embodies governmental approval being, as it will be, an accepted and acceptable part of the annual fête. And the committee members, having refreshed their glasses of Pastis once more, are astute enough to know that this idea sounds like an opportunity for the quiet and well-behaved folk of tiny Cabannes to finally get one over on that cosmopolitan crowd of intruders in neighbouring St Remy. After the briefest of discussions, which largely consist of everyone sagely repeating 'meh bah' a number of times, the motion is carried.

The committee members are quite overcome with the evening's proceedings. With a new initiate and the problematic demise of Henri, the paella provider, things were always going to be tricky. However, they have carefully manoeuvred their way through the agenda and have already made two successful and major changes to the fête programme. Some folk present in the upstairs room consider that their accomplishments are more than adequate for one evening and, tipping back the last of the Pastis, feel it's time for a proper drink. However, Christophe calls their attention to his father who has been sitting quietly throughout the proceedings waiting his turn.

An air of despondency falls over the group. It would be ill-mannered to turn Monsieur Martin away and it would, furthermore, entail a reconvening at some other time in order that the presentation can be heard. Another brief discussion ensues with more 'meh bahs' and a compromise is reached: they will send downstairs for a couple of bottles of the red stuff, listen to Monsieur Martin and scribble through any other business on the agenda.

Monsieur Martin reflects on his life which he has, hitherto, spent in minding his own business. He's a man who's had more to do with animals than humans; on the rare occasions that he's formed alliances with people, they have generally been with one person at a time, short, sharp and terminal, and almost always by chance. The one major exception to this is when he purposively and purposefully courted the girl who would become his wife. Prior to that, his companions comprised a troupe of performing poodles. And following his move down the lane that runs from the road between Noves and Cabannes, many years passed until Sophy and he became friends. One day, Phyllida and the partner who cannot be named became his neighbours when, inexplicably, they moved into a former remise belonging to Monsieur Regnier. That they became his very dear friends was really due to the polite generosity Monsieur Martin displayed in sharing his courgettes. That their friendship eventually allowed him to reach the point where he could begin his miniature riding school is a constant source of both disbelief and gratitude.

Of course, there have been two or three others along the way: there is Gerard who seems to demand little more from life than the opportunity to speak with horses. There was Monsieur Villiers who, despite upsetting the apple cart by falling in love with Madame Martin, only to upset another load of apples by disappearing, magnanimously offered professional help in engendering a relationship between Monsieur Martin and Clovis; and, naturally, there is Christophe. In the usual tradition, Monsieur Martin is about to discard the last of this extra populum in his life as soon as the fellow has permeated his thoughts. However, about to make his first public presentation, Monsieur Martin looks at Christophe a little more carefully.

He sees a man on a mission. He sees a young man who wants to be recognised and who needs to win something. Monsieur Martin feigns self- recognition and has no desire to win anything. Nonetheless, he realises that Christophe, who is neither educated nor articulate, has somehow managed to persuade a committee – a committee no less of which he is an initiate - that he has a jolly good idea. And Christophe, despite all the odds, has also made it possible for his father to be heard this evening. All things considered, Monsieur Martin feels he has a duty to himself and his friends and family. He takes a large swig of the red stuff and sets forth.

It could so easily have gone horribly wrong. Monsieur Martin is not a politician. Neither is he a part of this cabal of village elders who despise change. He has no recognition or articulation of the words that his son unexpectedly possesses so is unable to contextualise his idea in terms of benefits to the village. Monsieur Martin does what he has always done: he paints a simple picture devoid of hidden agenda and ulterior motives. This one portrays what the parade might look like with the inclusion of his small spotted ponies and the delight of the village children who are learning to ride.

By the time he's finished, the majority of the committee members are in tears. Part of this mass waterfall may be due to the most excellent wine that Monsieur, le Patron, has provided subsequent to the even more excellent Pastis. Cynics might argue that the committee members are anxious to be somewhere else that involves dinner. Official accounts will record that Monsieur Martin successfully reminded them of the values of a village fête that were certain to be passed down through the generations. The motion is unanimously passed, someone draws a line through any other business, and everyone adjourns to the bar to celebrate change.

Chapter Seventeen

These are heady days. Let us not forget where we are. The folk of Provence, who have a collective loss of memory when it comes to seasons past, welcome every spring as though it were their first. They rejoice in the decline of the bitter, sleep-disturbing mistral and applaud the advent of weather sufficiently warm enough to enable those first tentative meals taken outdoors under piercing blue skies. They delight in the emergence of almond blossom and they visit their churches to praise the unexpected arrival of the Mimosa which has not been seen since last year. They celebrate their luck in having been born in, or arrived at, such a place and time that promises the warmth that will sustain their well-being. And they forget how unbearably hot it will be in June.

Madame Martin is in her kitchen supervising Sophy who has recently exchanged her small child's jogging outfit for one of her new employer's miniscule aprons. To all intents and purposes things are going well. The labels are waiting to be neatly handwritten. The cloth caps and ribbon that Madame Lapin has persuaded her partner are necessary for purchases made by Americans (against Madame Martin's better judgement), sit waiting to adorn the shiny sterilised jars that have been polished to perfection. And into these, a batch of courgette and red pepper pickle, now resting in the expectation of a new home, will soon be decanted. Two wooden boxes of early apricots, which are currently being sourced from a neighbouring orchard to meet the increased demand for confiture, have just been delivered and require preparation. Sophy wonders how they will manage all these culinary demands between the two of them. Madame Martin has yet to explain to her sous chef that the arrival of yet another kitchen assistant is imminent. She wipes the meteorological and psychological sweat from her tiny furrowed brow in anticipation of the task ahead.

Christophe, who is naturally absent from the steaming kitchen, is both the cause of and solution to his mother's staffing problem. These days, Christophe is a man about town. Well, in reality, he's a man about Cabannes but he's fast becoming a renowned citizen of a wider area of Provence. Once the fête committee gave the quiz their blessing, it was impossible for Monsieur, le Patron, of the bar-tabac at St. Remy to turn down the invitation to the grudge match. He has rounded up the ex-pats and informed them that the honour of living in that town and its environs is at stake. There were, of course, murmurings of dissent, particularly when it was discovered that Cheesy Chips O'Connor would be replaced by Jean-Pierre Lucard's paella. However, the troops have rallied to the extent that they have hired a mini-van to transport them into the unknown.

Christophe, therefore, has his work cut out in ensuring that the organisation of this major event results in a night to remember. As well as maintaining a regular income from the potato packing day job, he has a team to coach, books to study, questions to formulate and music to reflect on. With regard to the last of these tasks, Christophe is struggling. To his knowledge, there isn't much of a selection to consider. All the Johnny Hallyday questions were asked previously in St. Remy and anyone else from the current music scene has yet to infiltrate the ears of Cabannes. Christophe has a plan: he will ask the partner who cannot be named for advice; the fellow seems to know a lot about this type of thing. The trouble is that all this responsibility leaves little time to develop his relationship with Netty. And Netty has begun to voice her unhappiness at finding herself last in a list of competing priorities.

Their assignations seem to solely comprise late night revision and testing of Christophe's latest knowledge garnered from his studies. They still haven't made a return visit to Plan d'Orgon at a time when Monsieur Villiers might be present and all the people that Netty might feel comfortable in asking – Monsieur Martin, Madame Martin and Madame Lapin – seem loathe to take her. Netty works in the evenings at the PMU bar so she has plenty of spare time during the day with little to occupy her. Christophe, who is now a man of ideas, has a eureka moment. He asks Netty if she would like to help Madame Martin in the kitchen chez lui. Netty will earn a small but extra income, Maman will be delighted that her only son has taken the trouble to resolve her staffing issues and Netty will have a greater opportunity to see her boyfriend. It's what the English call a win win situation. This isn't England. This is Provence and the only person who knows that Christophe's past and present girlfriends will soon be working together in a tiny kitchen is Madame Martin. She is underwhelmed to be in possession of such dangerous information.

Chapter Eighteen

The resident of Mas Saint Antoine known as Nanette is, once more, in an interesting lady dog condition. She is restless. Matters in this part of the canine world have not been helped by the arrival a female guest named Brigitta. Brigitta is a miniature daschund who, somewhat distressingly, given that it's her annual holiday, is also indisposed, so to speak. Or bark. For Nanette, it's too bad that there's an interloper on the scene. For Brigitta, who had been looking forward to a spot of Provençal sunbathing in her usual role of baby-demanding-sole-attention, the presence of Nanette is an affront: domestics should be neither seen nor heard. That both of them feel they are competing for something more than status, is a cradle of vitriolic confusion. For the last two days, this pair has been, or would be given half a chance, at each other's throats. The air is full of tension. And the scent of tension has now wafted over the manicured lawns, has bypassed the lavender bushes, has leapt over the precisely trimmed boundary hedges, has chosen to ignore the partner who cannot be named on his wooden chaise lounge, has edged its relentless way through the unexpected obstacle course comprising Phyllida's newly constructed raised vegetable beds, has overcome any trace of the blue fur monster and has finally arrived at a point between the tiny hurdles in Monsieur Martin's paddock where Clovis is taking his siesta.

The ears that belong to Clovis become suddenly erect. Surely history cannot be about to repeat itself? Clovis has about as much recall of history as the French have of the temperamental problems caused by the onset of summer. He has a now embryonic memory of an incident outside the ornate iron gates of Mas Saint Antoine last year. Clovis has no comprehension of the fact that, were it not for his previous escape bid, Madame Martin might now be comfortably reunited with her husband following her epiphany on La Montagnette; not the slightest inkling that Monsieur Villiers, who could have been ceremoniously dumped, despite his constant wooing of someone else's wife via the santons of Provence, would not now be lurking in Plan d'Orgon; and no concept of the implications for Christophe and his father-seeking girlfriend. In fact, were it not for doggy testosterone, this story would have terminated a long time ago and you, dear reader, newly inspired by all things French, would have moved on to Victor Hugo or Flaubert or any of those chaps. However, as we all know, like a magnetised boomerang, everything returns to money or sex; plus the fact that Clovis is exceedingly bored.

Clovis looks at Monsieur Martin and Gerard who are busy looking at the small spotted ponies which, in turn, are being studied from across the fence by the partner who cannot be named and who, momentarily, subsumed by the effects of the Buddhists, the Bulgarians and an unknown number of midday aperitifs, has lost his immediate point of reference. Clovis has had enough of this Provençal sangfroid. Something tells him not to make an obvious break for it. Instead, having long observed everyone else in these parts, he makes himself tiny to the point of invisibility and, like the thinnest of thin snakes, slithers quietly away.

If she ever even heard the knock at the door, Sophy, up to her pin-head elbows in courgette and red pepper pickle, shows no interest. Every step involved in the production of professional pickle demands undivided attention and maximum concentration, particularly on one's first day in paid employment. This business is too juvenile to be doing with spillage, wastage and poor spelling, especially when there's the possibility of an academic ex-lover making an appearance. Neither does Sophy appear to notice the look of alarm that crosses the already worried face of Madame Martin. The lady of the house is not in a hurry to open la porte. The lady of the house would rather do anything than open the door. A second knock. This time Sophy looks up from her work with mild interest. She knows that people rarely knock on this door; visitors are unexpected in these parts. The hand of Madame Martin is forced. She reaches the other side of the room whereupon the hand that is in the grip of an unknown entity takes it upon itself to open the door. Here is Netty stepping prettily indoors for her first day's work chez Martin. Here is Netty about to pleasantly greet the unknown young woman on the other side of the wooden table. And here is Sophy, motionless at the point of pickle entering another jar. Sophy, adept in the art of combining jogging and espionage knows only too well the identity of this visitor. The only thing moving in this temporarily-frozen-in-time kitchen is doing so in oh-so-slow motion as a large dollop of courgette and red pepper pickle descends silently to the floor.

Over at Mas Saint Antoine, things are by no means motionless, silent or frozen in kitchen-time: déjà vu has returned with a vengeance that is no longer waiting outside the ornate iron gates. Less than an hour ago, he was a giant wolf in dog's clothing. Now, the serpent-like Clovis has somehow slithered and slunk his cunning way under the boundary hedge and is celebrating an untold number of missed birthdays on the manicured lawn. To be fair, his entry onto the estate was helped greatly by Nanette and Brigitta who, whilst not consciously working as a team, had sensed his purposive but silent journey across the place where old, gnarled and diseased pear trees once grew. Eager to make the visitor welcome, the two girls, in a frenzy of whining, yapping and other excited and excitable noises that sounded the initial alarm to non-canine residents on the estate, pushed stones aside to scratch and dig a point of entry useful to their equivalent of Jean-Pierre Lucard. Despite the lack of a gold chain, silver trike and paella bearing gifts, Clovis has been greeted with all the veneration due a second coming.

The problem with juxtaposition of events inevitably means that some characters who jolly well ought to be involved in current affairs can become potentially bypassed. As the courgette and red pepper pickle arrives in an uninvited blob on the kitchen floor chez Martin, and as the also uninvited Clovis arrives chez Mas Saint Antoine to the delight of Nanette and Brigitta, one might wonder why people who have indirectly caused such havoc are missing in action. Christophe, for example, has chosen this precise moment in time to visit the partner who cannot be named with a view to obtaining advice regarding the musical round of the forthcoming quiz. A few days ago, the partner who may be of a litigious nature took a rare trip away from the lane that runs from the road between Noves and Cabannes in order to visit a Swedish furniture warehouse in Avignon. There is something of a contradiction within the partner's character: on the one hand, he is metaphorically laid back to the point of horizontal. On the other hand, as he is a closet ex-pat and thus not of French origin, all the practical laying back can only be accomplished on sleek wooden furniture. Currently, whilst the partner reposes on his home-made chaise lounge, Christophe, politely enquiring about the intricacies of Bulgarian music, is troubled by the design of a Swedish timber garden chair. Somehow, the bend in the so-called upright section doesn't seem to fit the curve of a French spine and Christophe, experiencing some pain, fidgets incessantly.

'Ever wondered whether the dharmas constitute reality', asks the partner?

'Are they a new band', Christophe replies, as he tries to slot himself into the chair?

In the only conceivable synchronicity that can occur between these two, who are so far removed from each other on all imaginable levels, they turn to view the driver of a vehicle that has suddenly appeared on the lane running from the road between Noves and Cabannes. From the neck that supports the head of a female whose hair has been newly bleached, a pale green silk scarf sporting butterfly motifs flies freely through an open window.

'It's that bloody feminist from the mediathèque', they both agree in joint resignation. The partner stirs himself to replenish hospitable glasses and attend to his library of Bulgarian music.

Back in the parklands of Mas Saint Antoine, the rampant wolf-dog is floundering noisily: initially delighted at the reunion with his darling Nanette, Clovis is mightily confused by the presence of the equally delightful and beautifully perfumed German guest. Even though the tourist is a little on the short side for his preferences, Clovis has literally no idea of where to begin as he darts from one to the other of the welcome party, baying, whooping, crying and yelping. The two girls, unimpressed with the lack of hard action, have, in a most unladylike manner, begun to argue furiously with each other:

'I saw him first', barks a furious Nanette. 'There's history between us'.

'I'm the paying guest. Get back to the kitchen', responds the baby-demanding-sole-attention as she nips unkindly at Nanette's ankles.

Nanette bears her vicious pristine teeth and goes for the jugular. Brigitta, experiencing virginal desire and agility, manages to initially dodge the canine molars and takes a lump from Nanette's drooping tail. The two competitors for the doggy world's Jean-Pierre Lucard roll savagely over and over the neatly manicured grass whilst Clovis, now relegated to the role of whimpering onlooker, sadly considers his lack of self-worth.

Meanwhile, this sorry turn of events is simultaneously reflected in the kitchen chez Martin. The identity and history of the unexpected and already apron-clad invitee soon became clear to Netty. Once cognisant of the situation, she quickly brushed aside the pleasantries assumed for the purposes of continued employment and assumed the vitriol, euphemistically referred to as passion, associated with those who originate south of the South. However, Sophy, formerly recognised as a small and quiet woman of no particular perspective on life, has transformed herself into an evil, shrieking harridan armed with an infinite supply of red pepper and courgette pickle. Saucepans, boiling pans, resting pans and polished jam jars have evolved into missiles in this theatre of war masquerading as a Provençal kitchen. Madame Martin, unaware of her new affinity with Clovis, cowers behind her husband's armchair, likewise considering her ineptitude in getting a job done.

Chapter Nineteen

Over in the garden on the other side of the fence that divides the land where once old, gnarled and diseased pear trees stood, some puzzled consideration is being given to the various unexpected noises that are drowning out the soothing sounds of the latest cd of Bulgarian gypsy music. Had he any time to think about it, and had he any notion of how he might extract himself from the imprisoning Swedish chair, Christophe, who has already decided that Kalman Aleksander and his band might be a little too avante garde for both Cabannes and St. Remy, would have politely left some time ago. As it is, he's stuck; fortuitously, however, with a large glass of something fairly decent in his hand.

The blue fur monster, having been, up to this point, seeking respite from the heat in the forbidding rainforest of darkness, has also decided it's time to investigate local matters. Above the melee, the Norwegians can hear the detested and detestable Clovis. They can hear he's suffering. Sick of the Bulgarians and the boredom eventually experienced by all who are 'in charge', they too are looking for action. In unspoken agreement, they also metamorphose into a silent crawling entity and journey towards Mas Saint Antoine.

A selection of butterflies amassing around her recently de-wrinkled neck, Madame Lapin has arrived in the kitchen which is the source of her increasing business acumen. To say chaos reigns would be trite. To say this venue represents a professional, but obviously non-capitalist, means of production would be to destroy all the Marxist-Feminist ideology that underpins her raison d'être. There are women fighting and women cowering. Food, in some shape or form lines the crumbling kitchen walls. Jars are empty or smashed and pans lay bent and broken on the ancient floor tiles where a once subservient woman served her man without a suspicion of inequality. In a darkened corner, two young females are writhing unattractively, over, apparently, a non-existent man. Madame Lapin is horrified and dives into the brawl.

At Mas Saint Antoine, those distressed guests who have not returned to their rooms in order to pack their bags and reconsider their online table d'hôte reviews, have re-grouped in a cosmopolitan semi-circle around the dog fight, each shouting their own advice in a variety of languages. Brigitta's mother is particularly vociferous: simultaneously weeping in despair whilst urging the baby-soon-to-be-a-woman-daschund on to victory. This appalling scene is interrupted on three counts: firstly, as is to be expected, Louise, followed by Olivia the cleaner, arrives with distracting trays jammed with glasses of rosé, saucers of herb encrusted olives from last year's crop and tiny garlic-covered croutons. Secondly, as might also be anticipated, Louise's husband, having recently discovered that this year's model lawn mower possesses an extraordinarily efficient device for emergency stops, appears on the scene wielding a large stick. And lastly, but most impressively, a blue fur monster of Norwegian provenance metamorphoses under the boundary lavender bush to take aim at poor Clovis. Clovis, with one last consideration of missed opportunities, and mindful of small spotted ponies and hurdles, jumps over the fence with a degree of athleticism not previously noted upon his slithering entry to the world of desperate lady dogs.

Christophe, aware of shrieks, shouts and weeping emanating from chez Martin, has downed the last dregs of his unidentified aperitif, has somehow managed to extract himself from his Scandinavian imprisonment and has set off in the direction of human distress chez lui. Here he will meet with Monsieur Martin and Gerard who have also been alerted to some, as yet unknown, cataclysmic event occurring in the kitchen. Thus there are two meetings of the many in close proximity this afternoon. On one hand, as we know, a group of virtual strangers are gathered around an indefinite number of dogs and cats behind the ornate iron gates on the road between Noves and Cabannes. On the other hand, a selection of folk who know each other only too well have amassed in a Provençal kitchen in order to ascertain a suitable response to a problem of epic proportions apparently caused by the production of red pepper and courgette pickle.

The partner who cannot be named, impervious of and oblivious to events irrelevant to the world of sixth century Buddhism, acoustics that fail to relate to Kalman Aleksander, uncaring of online table d'hôte scores, in no way knowledgeable of the concept of women fighting over a man and sufficiently warmed by the Provençal sunshine which determined his move here, not to mention a mind numbing number of aperitifs, stays where he is. That is, until a large animal reminiscent of a wolf rushes through the raised vegetable beds followed closely by a blue fur monster. They trample upon the summer flowers and head for the forbidden and foreboding rainforest whose thoroughfare is helpfully indicated by a number of colour coded signs.

The carnage and confusion in the kitchen chez Martin is such that it's impossible to know where to start. Therefore, the simplest thing is to bypass it all and hurry on to the end of this unfortunate turn of events. We know there will be long nurtured recriminations and grudges but, once the remains of the pickle and the broken jars have been swept up and disposed of, and the walls have been washed down and disinfectant applied, and all the participants and late arrivals have sat down around the newly scrubbed table with a glass of something beneficial, these concerns will, eventually, fester only silently in the thoughts of the main characters. Likewise, once lady dogs have been returned to their rightful owners and holes in the manicured lawns of Mas Saint Antoine have been suitably re-turfed, and guests have been placated, all will return to as near to normalcy as can be mustered in the South. The biggest problem is over at Phyllida's place.

The partner who cannot be named and who, thus far, has been known for his ability to let the entire world sweep over the top of his silver haired head, is very upset; so much so that he has discarded his chaise lounge, has abandoned his book of 6th century Buddhist philosophy, has allowed Kalman Aleksander and his band to become more than a little repetitive and has headed off for the original garden, also known to us as the rainforest. This action, in fact any spontaneous action on his part, is hitherto unknown. Now we see a side to his character which has never before been witnessed; at least not within these pages. Shouting and cursing in an admirable number of languages, including Latin, emanates from within the bamboo and tamarisks. Barking and mewing, yelping and hissing, the like of which until only recently filled this darkened place, have suddenly subsided. And Phyllida, who has been previously and quietly ensconced in her own kitchen, doing something interesting with a mango, a pineapple and a saucepan of coconut milk, rushes out into the weakening sunshine to lovingly scoop up an armful of terrified blue fur. Yet again, Clovis is seen slinking off, this time in any direction that does not involve cats, dogs or neighbours of any nationality.

Chapter Twenty

We don't generally hear much of or from Phyllida. She also likes a quiet life; a life that involves a semi-naked neighbour with an excess of large courgettes, a close friend who runs a successful table d'hôte business, a partner she has forgotten how she ended up with in Provence but whom she adeptly skips around when necessary and four perfect blue Norwegians who repose on her bed every night. If you thought the partner avoided trouble, you haven't considered the skills of Phyllida who, having now repaired superficial damage to her own beloved plants and those in the gloomy garden behind the remise, decides that if the geniality of the South is to be perpetuated, this day will be best terminated by inviting everyone, excluding Clovis, Nanette and Brigitta, for the aperitif.

It's a splendid idea, news of which soon permeates the environs. Over at chez Martin, those present are in a new state of confusion: although Monsieur and Madame Martin have been friends with their neighbours for several years, they have, from a slight timidity at the cosmopolitan mix generally present, never before crossed the threshold into the garden where twinkling lights hang from the old Plane tree. Despite having witnessed many aperitifs being taken by visitors of one nationality or another, they have yet to taste the cocktails or crudités. They have no comprehension of any intricacies that might be involved in multicultural parties. But, let's be clear, Provençal life down the lane that runs from the road between Noves and Cabannes is currently in so much turmoil, there's no way they're turning down this invitation. So, Monsieur and Madame Martin, Christophe, Gerard, Netty, Sophy and the feminist from the mediathèque, and Louise, her husband and the parents of Brigitta, all make their ways to this oasis of bonhomie.

It's a warm and wonderful evening, typical of many past and yet to arrive in Provence. No-one present mentions any of the afternoon's events and everyone takes ample share of all offered refreshments.

As the glorious sun drops slowly behind the trees that border the land of Phyllida and her partner, as the song of the cicadas gently subsides, as the butterflies disappear to be replaced by the first suggestion of the waking owls and the singing frogs, our thoughtful hostess refills glasses with Pastis and rosé for those of the company with more traditional tastes and with strange cocktails for the more daring. And finally, as the Bulgarians are dismissed at last, the mellow blues of the man formerly from New York, latterly from Isle sur la Sorgue, and currently to be seen and heard in St. Remy on market days, permeate the souls of all who are gathered here to meet the oncoming night: the velvet voice of Leonard Blair reaches out from the cd player inside the remise and subtly enhances the mass bonding in this most delightful of settings.

Monsieur Martin and Gerard discuss the participation of the small spotted ponies in the parade at the forthcoming fête with the partner who cannot be named. The partner is so excited at this news that he offers to help on the day. Christophe, anxious to avoid being seen as favouring one or other of the young women present, makes an effort to engage Louise's husband and Brigitta's father with ideas he has for a special round in the quiz, also at the fête. And Phyllida, Louise and Brigitta's mother are, based on their individual and collective experiences, busy advising Sophy and Netty on the best ways to deal with men. Regardless of subject and context, everyone has something to say and Phyllida's garden basks in ambience. It's a perfect setting for Madame Martin to finally enjoy a longed-for, non-business-type conversation with her friend and confidante, Madame Lapin.

Madame Martin and Madame Lapin have never drunk the Mojito before and always open to new taste sensations, they are very much impressed by the simplicity of the cocktail. Of course, Madame Martin is a veritable wizard with herbs but it has never occurred to her to add a bunch of mint to a large container of white rum. What other ingredients the sugared glasses of these two ladies might contain provides a source of interested discussion as they sip and suck on their red and white straws. In fact, thanks to Phyllida's generosity, it takes until the arrival of the third Mojito before the two business partners have reached a consensus which, incidentally, is not far from the truth. Their conversation, slightly more slurred than at the outset, but exceedingly genial, moves onto other matters. Of course, slurred conversation is very often accompanied, if not directly caused by, loose tongues. And loose tongues very often result in conversation over which the numbed brain plays catch-up.

With some bravado, but not without politeness, Madame Martin asks Madame Lapin about her newly acquired style. In particular, Madame Martin would like to know whether her friend and confidante has been especially inspired by some life-changing event that has caused her to drop the outward appearance of an old school feminist. Or perhaps she wishes to attract something in the order of change? Madame Lapin regards Madame Martin with a look that indicates indecision in one who may have a secret, removes the red and white straw from her Mojito and takes a large confidence boosting swig.

'Actually,' Madame Lapin explains quietly and carefully, as if speaking to a small child, 'being a feminist doesn't necessarily mean you have to abstain. If you know what I mean', she adds?

Madame Martin has no idea what her friend means but she nods sagely. She can't remember ever having this type of for-your-ears-only tête-à-tête with a woman before and is becoming eager to share her own secrets. Phyllida, Louise and Brigitta's mother however, having run out of advice for the younger women, and having overheard Madame Lapin, despite that lady's words being not meant for public consumption, know exactly what she means and have turned their full attention to the purveyors of jam and pickle.

'It's a man then', says Louise.

Madame Lapin looks around to make sure that none of the men present are listening. Having now formed a single mass of authoritarian debate on how to beat the British and American ex-pats at their own game, the men are not listening to the group on the other side of the gender divide. Emboldened by the Mojito and the interest of her audience, Madame Lapin finally spills the beans. Yes, it's a man; a man worth more than a mere consideration of appearance; a man worth developing a style for. A man from south of the South no less; dark and swarthy as a man should be.

'How did you meet', enquires Phyllida?

'Quite unexpectedly', comes the reply. 'We met when my pet rabbit was unwell'.

Madame Martin had no idea that Madame Lapin owned a pet rabbit. At another time and on another day Madame Martin might have considered an animal particularly well-suited to mustard, onions and a saucepan as a stupid choice for a pet. However, this is not another time or another day. This is Phyllida's garden at nearly nine in the evening on this auspicious date which Madame Martin, despite the Mojito, thinks will be forever etched in her memory. She tries to blot out what she knows is coming next but fails.

'A vet', asks Netty who also feels something important is imminent?

'Mais oui', Madame Lapin continues, 'a new man, in more than one sense. The man in Plan d'Orgon'.

'What's his name', demands the excited Netty?

'Monsieur Villiers'. It is Madame Martin who speaks so sadly.

Part Four

Chapter Twenty~One

Just when you think that the whole of Provence might explode in the increasingly oppressive heat of high summer that has wrapped itself around our little company and tied them in an unfathomable knot, a thunderstorm crashes its way into the lives of those whose tempers have already been frayed beyond repair. Of course, l'orage is not a widespread phenomenon but a localised and dangerous event. For example, one end of the road between Noves and Cabannes sits in the sunshine. However, a field of melons at the opposite end is decimated in minutes by a fierce and unwieldy hailstorm. When the mistral arrives, it can last for days but afterwards the air will be purified, the firmament will startle in blue and the world will be cleansed. In comparison, minutes after the storm has passed, the sky remains grey and the affairs of a limited number of people will be much as they were previously; although, for some, there is added and unexpected destruction to deal with.

So it was following that short-lived period of turmoil in the gardens off the road that runs between Noves and Cabannes. Nonetheless, within this particular microcosm, kitchen walls have now been washed and broken glass disposed of; holes in lawns have been repaired and guests appeased; online table d'hôte ratings have been rectified; raised flower and vegetable beds have been restored; rainforests have been reclaimed; dogs and cats are subdued; and the Mojito, having gained in unanticipated popularity, has been responsible for the non-meteorological disappearance of all available mint in the locale. The only person who is experiencing permanent injury is Madame Martin. Unlike that patch of land where, only yesterday, golden melons flourished with promise, the afflicted damage is not apparent to others: as ever, she's keeping her thoughts to herself. Life continues.

In the kitchen chez Martin and in Gaston's back bedroom there has been a reassessment of enterprise strategy. Too much, too soon is now a mission stating mantra to be avoided in hindsight: the prospective move into Isle sur la Sorgue has been temporarily abandoned. Business is booming but not sufficiently to warrant all this anxiety, cost and upheaval. Madame Lapin, newly unfettered by past secrets, is astute enough to recognise the potential confusion caused by excess diversification and the advantages of exclusivity.

'Make them come to Eygalières', she argues. 'If they can't get there, they'll have to buy the stuff online'. It's a simple enough philosophy but one that underpins their very business objectives: spread the word sufficiently and folk will be spreading the jam and pickle far and wide. The only exception to the confinement of confiture in Eygalières is the one-off stall that Madame Lapin and Madame Martin will hold at the artisan fair during the forthcoming annual fête in Cabannes.

In order for these marketing plans to mature, there has been a meeting of the ways between Netty and Sophy which can only be conducive to business in the jam and pickle department. For the worldly wise reader, there was no apparent reason for these two to end up at each other's throats. Reader, try not to be so worldly wise: it's not good for you. Don't think big time. These are geographically challenged young women with not much in the way of choice when it comes to young men. And they are the same as young women universally who, faced with this type of shortage, need to keep their options open. They're over it and, much to Christophe's confusion, are now the best of friends: friends who compare notes over their respective roles in the kitchen chez Martin. Sadly, the 'get-over-it' attitude is a little trickier for the more mature woman. It's not as easy to be stoic when no-one knew you had an 'it' to get over in the first place.

And Christophe, when he's not worrying about the women in his life, has, regarding the grudge match, been reinvigorated by preparations for Round Three: the life of Jean Moulin. He knows only too well that most people avoid Plan d'Orgon. Further, the ex-pats know no-one who lives there and, even if they've ever heard of the place in their closeted existence, they're unlikely to have travelled outside the eternal triangle of Avignon, Arles and St. Remy. Christophe has been studying the mural at St. Andiol with some relish. He has made copious notes, copies of which he has discretely distributed to relevant, but as yet, unimpressed parties at the PMU bar in Cabannes. Further, the music round, which was latterly troubled by the possible inclusion of Kalman Aleksander and his band, now comprises a number of questions based on that famous blues singer, originally from New York, but lately of Isle sur la Sorgue, Leonard Blair. The ex-pats will have seen and heard him at the Wednesday market in St. Remy but it's unlikely they will have asked who he is. Things are looking good.

Monsieur Martin and Gerard have also been preoccupied with preparations to the extent that courgettes, peppers and tomatoes have, largely, been left to their own irregular horticultural devices. The horse owner and the horse whisperer have ensured that all members of the annual fête committee, excluding Christophe who has no known or claimed offspring, will now have an undersized family member present in the parade. Hurdles have been temporarily discarded as the small spotted ponies and their riders practise walking in polite lines around the paddock.

Meanwhile, Madame Lapin, having donned an unlikely apron to protect her halter- necked silk chemise and second-skin leggings, has joined Netty and Sophy in the kitchen chez Martin. Under the quiet supervision of the lady of the house, these three are busy filling and dressing the jars which will promote the soon-to-be-famous confiture and pickle at the artisan fair. After numerous discussions, the business finally has a name to be embossed upon the labels and website: Les Deux Bonnes Madames. Monsieur Martin says it reminds him of something familiar that he can't quite put his finger on. Sophy and Netty want to know where they stand in the numerical scheme of things. Gaston asks how he's supposed to fit such a long banner on the website. Christophe says it sounds like a whorehouse. The partner who cannot be named has no opinion. Clovis whines.

Chapter Twenty-Two

Thus we eventually arrive at the weekend where Cabannes is en fête...two heady days of celebrations commencing with the artisan market on Saturday morning. Friday evening sees a culmination of the week-long sweltering hotbed of activity at the bottom of the lane that runs away from the road between Noves and another village currently adorned with flags. Madame Lapin is suitably dressed for the weather in a fetching pale pink camisole and a long, flowing fuchsia coloured skirt; but inappropriately clothed, according to Madame Martin, for last minute dealings with jars of peach jelly. This concoction is les deux bonnes madames' latest and extraordinarily versatile product. Peach jelly, in all its loveliness, when spread upon a piece of fresh baguette, is a far lighter alternative to that heavy chocolate spread so secretly adored by the thin housewives of France. And peach jelly, when discretely placed alongside an unsuspecting slice of saucisson, reflects the very essence of Provence. Yes, peach jelly is the way forward this weekend when it will be inaugurated at the artisan fair.

As it's early evening, Netty is behind the PMU bar in Cabannes serving the first of the already-in-holiday-mode revellers. Sophy, however, is still present in the kitchen chez Martin turning her child-like hands to all sorts of necessary tasks. Once all the jars have been dressed, polished and placed in boxes they will be loaded onto the back of the pick-up truck. At this point in time, Sophy, with some ambivalence, will jog her way back to the embracing arms of Dr Giraud in Noves. Madame Lapin and Madame Martin, meanwhile, will transport the boxes of jars to Cabannes where they will be unloaded and invited to pass the night in the reception area of the mediathèque. This will be secured against the possible intrusion of pickle thieves and jam robbers. The two madames will then drive the pick-up truck back out of Cabannes towards Noves and down the lane that winds away from anything that smacks of excitement. At chez

Martin, Madame Lapin will drive her own car, which will contain Madame Martin, back up the lane, along the road from Noves and once more into Cabannes where the two entrepreneurs will take a glass of something celebratory in the PMU bar. Monsieur Martin will join them later. Madame Martin wonders whether anyone else will be joining their small party. In particular, anyone else arriving from the direction of Plan d'Orgon who she might not have seen for some time.

At present, Monsieur Martin is still in the paddock with Gerard, the small spotted ponies and, most auspiciously, the partner who cannot be named who has, for the first time ever, crossed to the other side of the fence that divides the land where old gnarled pear trees once stood. The partner has always admired the small spotted ponies. However, since they arrived directly in his line of sight, once the paddock was completed, he became entranced. When Gerard also appeared and began to whisper ancient folk tales of the Camargue into the tiny ears of equine heads that turned in interest, the man of a possibly litigious nature became spellbound. And when the dear little children from Cabannes finally took their places on the backs of the small spotted ponies, well – the partner was hooked. Recall, if you will dear reader that during the temper-calming, truth-spilling aperitif that Phyllida arranged after the non-meteorological storm, the partner expressed a heartfelt desire to help Monsieur Martin and Gerard in the parade. Now, pony-like, he has crossed the hurdle that comprises the barrier between the neighbouring gardens and is busy platting the mane of a horse with no name. (In truth, the small spotted ponies do have names but they are of ancient, sacred and mythological derivation known only to themselves and the horse whisperer). The partner is unconcerned, being also one who cares not to share personal information such as identity. Tomorrow, he will leave all thoughts of Buddhist philosophy, Swedish furniture and Norwegian felines behind as he joins Monsieur Martin and Gerard in the important business of the parade.

Christophe and the rest of Team PMU2 are in the room above that prestigious venue engaged in a spot of last minute revision prior to some preparatory drinking below. All over Cabannes the usual scheme of order and direction is turned on its head as blockades are erected to prevent cars interrupting the parade and barriers are installed to avert citizens and visitors from being trampled on by the black bulls of the Camargue. In the square, the market stall frames are pieced together in readiness for tomorrow's artisan fair. Down the road and round the corner in the car park at Intermarché, the wooden stand that will, for two days, become the provenance of Jean-Pierre Lucard, his paella, his hot plate and all of his many other attractions, is almost erect. Close at hand, men are currently bringing out the long wooden tables and benches which will comprise the communal dining area where the good and not so good people of Cabannes will, along with their guests, feast after the bulls have flattened anything in their path on Sunday. Tomorrow, at une bonne heure, an area in front of the tables will be cordoned off in anticipation of the dancing that will take place to the accompaniment of a Johnny Hallyday tribute band late into Sunday night. It's fortunate that, as we know, no-one in France works on a Monday morning.

Chapter Twenty-Three

Saturday morning sees les deux bonnes madames behind their stall on which a delectable array of produce is displayed. They are surrounded by a diverse range of locally sourced goods sufficient to make proud Cabannes the potential centre of all things artisan. There is exquisite and delicate jewellery the like of which has never before graced these environs. Here is Pierre with his hand-carved wooden pictures, each containing emblems of Provence such as sunflowers and sprigs of lavender. Representatives from the Frigolet Abbey have brought small bottles of their dangerously green liqueur. Annie is attempting to manage a group of women who are trying on her multi-coloured bandanas and Jean-Claude is tempting other ladies with his naturally scented soaps. François has travelled over from Cavaillon with a van load of his reproduction photographs of village interiors, along with pictorial memories of the glory days when the Tour de France contestants dared to traverse Les Alpilles. People are spilling out of the PMU bar with their tiny, tiny cups of expresso. The sun, which will peak unwaveringly as the parade passes later, is currently warming the very souls of the folk of Cabannes and a surprising number of visitors. Were it not already a word of national origin, then the French would have to invent a name for this delicious moment. They would call it bonhomie.

Madame Martin is inwardly struggling to feel a sense of bonhomie. In this, she was somewhat helped at last night's preamble by the non-appearance of people claiming to have travelled from Plan d'Orgon. Strangely, Madame Lapin seemed unconcerned by the absence of anyone in the veterinary business and the other bonne Madame suspects that an arrival could be imminent. Madame Lapin has certainly taken some trouble with her appearance this morning. The once aspiring feminist seems to be in denial of previous ideology and, dressed in an off-the-shoulder number, sports a red rose in her hair .The equally attractive peach jelly is to the fore of the display and having been initially treated with a degree of suspicion has, on tentative tasting, been followed by a clamour of purchases. This has taken Madame Martin's mind off all things illicit until a very macho voice intercedes.

'Ma Cherie, how can I have found something so delightful in this unknown place?'

Madame Martin is conscious of her partner quivering and is loath to turn the eyes contained in her tiny face upwards. But she does. And those large, once-acrobatic eyes, on turning, meet with another pair of piercing green eyes that fill a brown face which is shaped by a head of silver hair. And the face of the head that is clothed in silver sits on a brown neck which reaches down through an unbuttoned pale blue shirt under which a gold chain sparkles. And the pale blue shirt meets the grand shiny buckle of a brown leather belt which holds a pair of blue denim jeans in place above the black, slightly heeled boots of an image that is shrouded in the combined scents of expensive after-shave and hot onions. Jean-Pierre Lucard is in town. And all the women of Cabannes, like a gigantic fondue into which they have been absorbed, melt en masse.

Madame Lapin, like the Reines-Claudes, is usually contained. This is not, however, a usual day. Fluttering her eyelashes and brushing imagined stray wisps of hair from her face, which is now colour co-ordinated with the rose behind her ear, she is unrecognisable as the once aspiring feminist from whose path the men of Cabannes shrunk in both derision and fear. She has fallen from her stern, philosophical, self-made pedestal under the weight of flattery. Although, according to Madame Martin's astute observations, it remains less than clear to whom or what the paella purveyor has directed his comment. It could, of course, be this woman whose off-the-shoulder chemise is currently nearer her elbow than its previously higher resting place. On the other hand, as Jean-Pierre Lucard is treating his peach jelly-covered slice of saucisson with more apparent relish than is contained in any of the jars on display, the object of his attention and affection might originate in the combination of local fruit and dead pig. And even more disconcerting for Madame Martin is the no-getting-away-from-it fact that JPL is looking directly at her.

'Darling', says the embodiment of desire around whose planetary attributes the females of Cabannes are currently orbiting. But we are never to learn what this Provençal play-boy is about to say, or, indeed, to whom the next line might be directed, for into this moment of artisan interrupting confusion comes another unassuming actor.

'Mesdames, bonjour; ça va bien?' And it's clear that this greeting is addressed, with a possible hint of embarrassment, to both of the ladies behind the stall. Two female heads turn in synchronicity and look down on the small, dark and swarthy intruder who clearly originates from south of the South but who, latterly, has arrived from the environs of Plan d'Orgon. For different reasons, neither of the bonnes madames appears particularly pleased at the untimely arrival of Monsieur Villiers. Madame Lapin, were she English, would be observed to gird her loins. It's not an expression familiar in Cabannes but we can see that she's trying to pull herself together and bring a sense of decorum to the occasion. She looks wistfully at the space that Jean-Pierre recently inhabited but, wiping the remains of peach jelly from one of his delicious cheeks, he's already on his way to the car park at Intermarché to cook the first batch of paella accompanying, Camargue-originating rice. Another missed opportunity she, and many others, sadly concur.

Madame Martin, meanwhile, is not girding her loins. At least not in an overt fashion. The woman who has nothing to show for past secrets and emotional turmoil, apart from a mobile telephone that never rings, is more than a little abrupt towards persons of a veterinary bent. Even though Monsieur Villiers has presented himself to both ladies, Madame Lapin attempts an introduction between the vet and her business partner. Madame Lapin is still in a state of psychological and physical disarray caused by an unanticipated excess of male entrances and exits. Very probably she has forgotten, if she ever knew, that Monsieur Villiers was once a regular visitor chez Martin. In truth, it's highly likely that she's unaware that the dark and swarthy man from south of the South once forged a meaningful relationship between Monsieur Martin and a dog. And without a bean spillage, there's no reason for her to know that this same man had been responsible for relationship formation of other kinds down the bottom of the lane.

'Monsieur Villiers', she begins, 'I would like to introduce...'

'I know Monsieur Villiers very well', the other bonne madame interrupts.

Madame Lapin is somewhat taken aback by the tone of her partner's voice. Ditto for Monsieur Villiers who, feeling his presence is not currently desired in front of the jam and pickle stall, suggests all three meet at the close of the artisan fair in order to enjoy the parade.

'Whatever', says Madame Martin as she moves to serve a new cohort of customers.

'Certainement', says Madame Lapin as she rearranges her rose, pulls the down-to-the-elbow strap back up to its original off-the-shoulder position and reassumes a demeanour appropriate to an entrepreneur.

Despite more than agreeable results in the sales department of the jam and pickle stall, and the enthusiasm shown for the peach jelly, an unhappy air of the unknown hovers dubiously over the two bonnes madames. Madame Lapin cannot understand her partner's earlier apparent hostility towards Monsieur Villiers. On the other hand, Madame Martin is having difficulty in reconciling Madame Lapin's almost indifference at the appearance of the vet. At midi, the two women sit down to a light lunch comprising bread, saucisson and a spoonful of peach jelly washed down with half a chilled bottle of rosé; which is about the only thing behind the stall that has kept its cool this morning. Although it's a good marketing ploy to be seen eating their own produce, there's no doubt that at least one of these ladies who lunch would have secretly preferred a taste of what's on offer over at the Intermarché car park.

Chapter Twenty-Four

At two of the clock, the bell that rests in its mistral-proof grating within the church tower announces the start of the parade. Madame Martin and Madame Lapin, having finished their midday meal and packed their remaining jam jars into the boot of the latter's car outside the mediathèque, have secured an excellent viewing point in front of the square which is now empty of artisan fair stalls. They are accompanied by Sophy and Dr Giraud who has managed to leave his stethoscope in Noves on the basis that no-one in France is allowed to be ill on a day when the local village is en fête. Netty has also succeeded in leaving her position behind the PMU bar and has temporarily joined the group as has Christophe and Team PMU2 who have no-one to serve them. Monsieur Villiers, who, let's be fair, has played such an important role in the past affairs of some of our protagonists, and who secured this ideal vantage point in the first place, seems annexed to the end of the party like an unwanted contingency plan.

To the sound of hearty and genuine cheering, the parade processes towards the square. In the lead, naturally, is the mayor, his good wife and assorted officials transported on what appears to be a mediaeval farm-cart which is drawn by two equally ancient heavy horses. Driving this band of importance is an even more antediluvian being who looks as if he might have been playing this role since time immemorial. Which, indeed, he has. Behind them, in a smaller carriage, comes this year's Miss Cabannes: a delightful stick insect of about seventeen years of age at whose flowing locks Madame Lapin, having temporarily regained her raison d'être, might have been observed to spit. Christophe sneers at the older woman and leers at the younger. But this momentary difference of opinion is quickly overcome by the section of the parade that follows the beauty queen.

Here, for the first time ever in the history of the parade, comes a tiny troupe of immaculately turned out small spotted ponies. At the front is a short unassuming gentleman who is clothed in an aura of pride. In one hand, he holds the rein of the largest of the ponies which, on its back, carries the well-dressed daughter of the mayor. Both pony and child have assumed the stature of greatness. In Monsieur Martin's other hand is another lead on the end of which, a wolf, dressed in a red and white spotted neckerchief, trots as one who denies any previous untoward behaviour. Behind these, a man whose name is unmentioned and unknown, and who walks with the superiority of those who are unmentioned and unknown, but who is instantly recognised as a person of intellect, brings two more small spotted ponies, each bearing a person of restricted growth. Finally, a horse whisperer who has, at last, attained his childhood dream of appearing in an equine parade, manages four small spotted ponies and their riders, all of whom have succeeded in walking politely. Madame Martin and her party clap enthusiastically but, really, there is no need for such familial and social support as the crowds, adoring of this movable tableau of Provençal goodness, cheer with a never-before-seen patriotic will.

There are, naturally, others in this parade but Madame Martin et al have seen all that is necessary and retire to various quarters in preparation for attendance at the evening's quiz. Netty resumes her duties at the PMU bar for a spot of tidying up and organising of tables. Sophy and Dr Giraud return to Noves for a spot of who knows what. Christophe, surprisingly, accompanies maman back down the lane that runs between Noves and the site of potential evening glory. Madame Lapin and Monsieur Villiers wander off together into the unknown, with more enthusiasm on the part of one than the other. Monsieur Martin, Gerard and the partner who cannot be named, having deposited tiny but successful riders into the arms of adoring parents, will shortly bring home the now illustrious troupe of small spotted ponies. Phyllida, who is a silent and unseen observer of all of the matters hitherto mentioned, prepares a surprise aperitif.

Chapter Twenty~Five

Madame Martin sits quietly under the plane tree in Phyllida's garden with a small glass of rosé to hand. The little wooden table that Phyllida has helpfully provided for her glass and a dish of olives is otherwise occupied by a large mass of Norwegian blue fur which possesses a head at either end. Another smaller bundle of cat sits on Madame Martin's lap which, given the minimal space provided by said lap, rather swamps the jam and pickle purveyor. Madame Martin, however, seems unconcerned by possible feline suffocation: she is reflecting, yet again, on the bigger things in life. Measured against her smallness, this includes almost everything. In particular, Madame Martin is thinking about her husband. She has been listening to Phyllida singing the praises of the partner who cannot be named. Phyllida is enormously proud of the partner's contribution to this afternoon's parade. The partner, as we know, rarely leaves either of his gardens so Phyllida is delighted that he has had this opportunity to give something to both Monsieur Martin and to the village.

It occurs to Madame Martin that she too was very proud of her own husband when she first observed that concise equine community processing towards her in Cabannes. Listening now to Phyllida, she realises how Clovis, Gerard and all the little riders played the parts that Monsieur Martin had designated to perfection. And that they had done so because of the high esteem in which they hold the often semi-naked tractor driver. And at this timely moment, Monsieur Martin appears at the gate with Gerard in order to join his wife and neighbours for the aperitif.

Christophe has already left for the PMU bar in order to be present when the ex-pat teams arrive. He finds Jean-Pierre Lucard has temporarily moved his paella pans into the back kitchen from whence a delicious, mouth-watering smell emanates. Naturally, Christophe, clutching two bottles of beer, bypasses Netty and makes straight for the domain of the grand chef in order to shake the hand of the mighty man. They exchange Bonsoirs and Christophe forwards a number of inane suggestions regarding the best way to poison the ex-pats. Jean-Pierre humours the idiot in front of him with a number of 'mais ouis', 'meh bahs' and a selection of 'voilas'. However, over and above the onion originating vapours, Jean-Pierre can smell the potential scent of monetary promise. There's no way that tonight's paella will be anything but the best. The ex-pats have money and hold plenty of parties. Jean-Pierre wants a piece of the lucrative fish and chicken action in St. Remy.

Monsieur, le patron also arrives bearing another two bottles of beer as do Thiery and Michel who, once more, comprise half of Team PMU2. The fourth member will, unexpectedly, be Dr Giraud who, via the for-old-times-sake routine, Sophy has coerced into bringing his scientific and medical knowledge to bear. Madame Martin, who was a member of the original PMU team, has been side-lined owing to the fact that, as her son sees it, she never has the opportunity to garner further general knowledge from television quiz shows now that she spends all her time either making or selling jam and pickle. Nonetheless, Madame Martin will be joining another team alongside Monsieur Martin, Phyllida's neighbour, Louise and the partner who cannot be named but who, as we recall, was the winner of the last match.

At seven o clock, the horn of a mini-bus in the square announces the arrival of the ex-pat contingent from St. Remy. Jean-Pierre Lucard, in a clean set of chef's whites, worn casually over a fitted pair of black and white checked trousers, takes his band of sycophants outside to meet and greet this party who, to most of the welcoming crew represent the enemy. Not so to Jean-Pierre Lucard however who switches his alert system up to DEFCON 3 and turns the charm offensive to full throttle. Despite their aversion to anything French or challenging, several of the women alighting the mini-bus are observed to fall into an immediate swoon. All relevant parties make their cosmopolitan way into the tricolour festooned bar for the aperitif.

Reader, it's unnecessary to account for this evening round by round. Most of the characters who have wandered through these pages without ending up in the psychotherapy unit of the Henri Duffaut Hospital in Avignon are present. Some form teams whilst others are mascots running back and forth to the bar to provide continuous liquid refreshment. Interestingly, the person nominated by Christophe to write and deliver the questions, based on his chosen themes, is Madame Lapin. Another secret of which Madame Martin was unaware but also, in the face of her current domestic reassessments, is uncaring. Perhaps Christophe was mindful of preventing accusations of bias in this choice. After all, in a nearly forgotten incarnation, Madame Lapin is, as we recall, a librarian. In the event, the lady has dressed for the occasion most thoughtfully. Or, possibly, she has dressed for one or two of the gentlemen present. Of these, Monsieur Villiers, who had seemed without friends earlier in the day, now forms a quiz-like allegiance with Gerard, Sophy and Phyllida. Anyone bothering to make an observation regarding this team might have dismissed them as possessing in-depth knowledge, but only in the animal department. And there are indeed two or three observers: Monsieur Martin and his son, despite being occupied at separate tables, are both seen to be shooting daggers of spite at the reappearance of the man from south of the South. The dark and swarthy person is also the recipient of quizzical looks from the direction of that diminutive being behind the bar. Netty had been at one end of the group who had watched the parade that afternoon and had not noticed a man of veterinary leanings leaning against those at the other end.

In her most auspicious role, Madame Lapin reigns supreme, batting off all queries or murmurs of dissent like irritating flies beneath her swat of superiority. At least during the first half of the match. Rounds one and two are uneventful but the third round, the life of Jean Moulin, is definitive. As Christophe has foreseen, no-one from the ex-pat contingent appears to have the faintest idea who Jean Moulin was, let alone any hidden knowledge of his accomplishments buried in their rarely used long-term memories. By the time the quiz is temporarily halted for nutritional refreshment, Christophe is certain his team is ahead of the game.

Jean-Pierre Lucard, having designated Netty and Monsieur, le patron, as supervised and subservient paella distributors, exchanges his chef's outfit for one more fitting to the occasion. Any occasion, actually. An outfit where the delights of his brown chest, sheathed in a subtle cloud of fine, sparkling silver hair and topped with the glitter of the precious metal that hangs around his even more precious neck, are displayed to the quiet envy of most of the men and the delight of all the ladies of a certain age. Each of the latter quivers in anticipation as Jean-Pierre bends down at every table to enquire after their well-being on tasting his paella; thereby offering a sneaky peak further towards the area that the brown leather belt with the shiny buckle holds in place. The ex-pats, without exception, are adamant that the paella is the best they have ever tasted. No-one dares to mention Cheesy Chips O'Connor.

Special attention is paid to Madame Lapin who Jean-Pierre singles out once he has distributed his business cards to this captive audience of potential clients. Madame Lapin, feeling that she has already forged an existence in the paella purveyor's conscience, plays it cool. She may be fluttering and brushing inside but, with half the room watching, her credibility as an intellectual quiz-master who can manage proceedings and people in an efficient and business-like manner is at risk. For one who, only a mere few months ago, was resolute in her dismissal of men, she has, apparently, assumed the ability to successfully juggle two simultaneous admirers with startling deft.

Monsieur Villiers, however, is observing these courtship rituals with some disdain. He also has one eye on Madame Martin who seems to be making determined efforts to avoid responding to his non-verbal communication. Just as Monsieur Villiers notices the absence of Monsieur Martin from his wife's table, and decides to move across for a few words, he is tapped on the shoulder.

'Haven't seen you around for some time'. Monsieur Martin's greeting is some way between a statement and a question. Either way, he has succeeded in throwing the vet off kilter. Monsieur Villiers launches into a garbled account of the employment opportunities in Plan d'Orgon, a half-hearted attempt at describing a tenuous liaison with a librarian, his pleasure at watching the small spotted ponies earlier in the day, his delight in seeing Clovis and finally resorts to the offer of another glass of rouge. Monsieur Martin remains unimpressed although does find it apposite to mention the splendid service he has received from the veterinary clinic at Chateurenard. He also looks around for some back-up from his son but Christophe has disappeared out of the bar in order to enjoy a nicotine intake and a digestif suitable for relieving the after effects of the paella. Thus, a hiatus is reached but is, fortuitously, temporary, due to the onset of the second half of the quiz.

Once again, there is nothing of consequence to report until the music round. Apart from Team PMU2, no-one in the bar appears to have an inkling of the subject matter, Leonard Blair, although there is much discussion to be overheard:

'Is he a relation of Tony?' This from the ex-pats.

'Tony who?' This from the French.

Madame Lapin waves her question paper dangerously with all the expertise of a librarian and threatens the noisier teams with immediate expulsion from the match. Team PMU2 have been brilliantly primed by Christophe, the academic. Christophe has, however, forgotten that Phyllida and the partner who cannot be named, both on opposing teams, have a sound knowledge of the blues singer, lately of Isle sur la Sorgue. In fact, so has anyone else who has recently taken the aperitif at Phyllida's place, especially since the demise of the Bulgarians.

Finally, papers are exchanged, answers are given and scores are totted up. At this point, it almost goes without saying that everyone, with the exception of the unnamed mini-bus driver, has enjoyed more than adequate French hospitality. In a way, therefore, it hardly matters to most people that Monsieur Villiers' team has somehow won the day. There are some important exceptions to this. And various folk are waiting on the outside of the PMU bar for an opportunity to share a few quiet words with the vet. Amongst these is, of course, Christophe who feels he has some old scores to settle on the part of his dear Maman.

Chapter Twenty-Six

It seems abundantly clear to everyone apart from Christophe that he may not have picked his moment well. Monsieur Villiers is surrounded by ex-pats who, having had their best night ever away from St. Remy, are effusive in their congratulations to the winning team leader. The prize-pot couldn't have gone to a better person they agree. And, having discovered that their hero is a vet from Plan d'Orgon, all gathered promise to bring their pooches and kitties henceforth into his caring domain. Now they've ventured into the wilds of Cabannes there's no stopping their adventurous spirit. Once the ex-pats discover exactly where Plan d'Orgon is, they'll be there tout de suite to visit Monsieur Villiers and, naturally, to see the memorial to the local and national hero, Jean Moulin. Christophe tries to break into the melee before breaking into Monsieur Villiers but is stopped on two accounts. Firstly, the crowd from St. Remy need to shake the hand of the person who has organised such a truly splendid evening. As there are so many of them this takes rather a long time. Christophe is torn. On the one hand, he has unfinished business with the vet, especially since he's been denied the glory of winning the grudge match. On the other hand, despite being a loser of sorts, these accolades are what he's dreamed of. He is, finally, a respected person of importance.

Another person who's been waiting to have a quiet word with Monsieur Villiers, and who is also responsible for stopping Christophe's dangerous advances, is the small person who has been behind the PMU bar all evening. It's the first opportunity Netty has had to question the man who, like her, is clearly from south of the South and she wants Christophe to make the introductions. Netty hasn't seen her father for many years; not since she was a smaller person. She owns no photographs but feels she may have experienced a sense of recognition. Sadly, Monsieur Villiers, who is not, as far as we know, looking for lost relatives, is unable to comprehend or help Netty who, let's face it, has also chosen a pretty bad time to reclaim a father. Monsieur Villiers, overwhelmed by the exuberant praise of the ex-pats, the dangerous threats of Christophe and the plaintive attempts of Netty to make conversation is at a loss. He asks Netty if the two of them could meet tomorrow before the bulls rush through the town. At this suggestion, the emotional ex-pats demand to be present at the following day's celebrations despite their collective lack of tickets for the communal meal.

Just as we, dear reader, the quiet observers, think this ridiculous, but potentially tear-jerking, situation couldn't get more complicated, a man with flowing silver locks and a fully unbuttoned shirt wades into the crowd. Jean-Pierre Lucard will be more than happy to sell an unlimited number of Sunday evening meal tickets to anyone who has ready cash; bearing in mind that there will, unfortunately, be a paella penalty of undisclosed euro for those that hadn't planned ahead. The ex-pats, who already own stomachs that are sinking under the weight of fish, chicken and hot onions, fall on Jean-Pierre with unabated thanks and instantly part with their money. Monsieur Villiers takes this opportunity to sidle off into the darkness with a view to seeking out the comforts that might be offered by the librarian. Madame Lapin, however, is in a pre-arranged and hidden location under the bell tower of the little church. Here is a woman who can recognise a non-veterinary promise when confronted by such.

The following day dawns quietly. All over Cabannes, along the roads that lead into the village, and down the lanes that run from the roads that fall out of that full-of-fête place, people are nursing sore heads. Even those who are generally more temperate in their alcoholic intake are, this sunny morning, feeling the effects of the night before. At Phyllida's place, those that are always so adept at pacing themselves forego the delights and bargains of the vide-grenier, preferring to stay in their beds. Naturally, Phyllida rises at une bonne heure to feed the Norwegians but is, once again, resting. Likewise, over at chez Martin, there is little discernible movement. Gerard is also up early to make sure the small spotted ponies are in good health and the sprinklers that water the lately ignored tomatoes, courgettes and Madame Martin's supply of fruit are switched on. He has also now returned to his bed. No-one in this increasingly secular world has ventured into the church which houses the little bell that helpfully announces doom, gloom and celebration. And no-one that we know of has made it as far as the vide-grenier. They are saving themselves for a restorative lunch-time aperitif followed by a spot of bull-watching. This is what the French mean these days when they say they're en fête.

Chapter Twenty-Seven

By one of the clock, having partaken of a minimal aperitif and a very light lunch, all of our protagonists have managed to convey themselves back into Cabannes. They are much improved in physical health and temperament since this morning and with the help of another small glass of rosé are eager to view the animals. The black Camarguaise bulls, which are currently contained in the Intermarché car park, far too close to a wooden stand for the paella purveyor's liking, rarely venture as far as Cabannes. In another cordoned-off area, insufficiently separated from the bulls according to EU legislation, the famous white horses, also from the Camargue, are waiting impatiently to do their work in this once-a-year venue. Reader, if you are inexperienced in this kind of entertainment, you may deduce that the job of the proud white horses, guided by the gardians, is to direct the bulls through the tiny streets of the village. In a way, this is true. However, make no mistake: this is an interactive event whereby the onlookers also play a role. And the role of the audience is to try to distract the proud white horses and their riders in order that the black bulls can outwit everyone and roam freely through the streets. It's a death wish of the Provençal variety.

The gardians, in their brightly coloured shirts and cowboy hats, are gathered in groups in the car park. They have already enjoyed the aperitif and, having recognised Jean-Pierre Lucard as a fellow Frenchman for all seasons, have taken a short break from speaking softly to their horses in order to fill themselves full of pre-bull running paella. The gardians are unaware that they are being closely observed by another whisperer of smaller proportions. Like so many others in this saga, Gerard is desperately seeking something. To be precise, like Netty, he's on the lookout for a father. Unlike Netty, Gerard has located a person of known paternal standing. He makes his tentative way between the fetlocks of the enormous horses, whispering as he goes. The chicken munching gardians turn in synchronicity as it suddenly occurs to them that their restless steeds have, with ears erect, become silent. They can see no apparent reason for this unusual change in equine behaviour until Gerard emerges, unannounced, from the makeshift corral. Even then, explanations remain unexplained until Franck, their leader, recognises the calming intruder.

'My boy', Franck exclaims, whereupon there is one of those emotional family reunions thus far absent in these pages. To cut a tall and short story in length, there is at least one happy and tidy ending for which, at last, there is no need to wait any longer. Cutting this long and short story even further, Franck, having remembered that Gerard is a horseman of certain proportions, invites his son to hop aboard and squeeze into the father's saddle behind him for the triumphal march. Gerard weeps openly but stops almost as soon as he's begun when his father instructs him to get a grip of the reins. Gerard, fearing a backlash of plumber-associated suggestions, gets a grip. Thus Gerard, having firstly been fortified with a dish of chicken, fish and Camarguaise rice, rides into Provençal history.

Wipe your eyes reader. There's glory to be gained at this juncture but not before the youth of Cabannes have set off fire-crackers, have ridden their bicycles in the path of marauding bulls and have leapt out from behind randomly placed lampposts, armed with wheelie bins, to grab the tails of passing animals of the bovine genre. The folk of Cabannes, post-aperitif, are seeking action. And the visitors from the environs of St. Remy are, after last evening's beating, looking to instil a spot of anonymous indecorum into events outside their comfort zone.

Phyllida, that animal-loving neighbour is horrified. In this, she is alone. Everyone else, irrespective of provenance, has joined the disruptive fray with enthusiasm. It's true that all the animals finally arrive at the once-a-year bullring, but not before a degree of carnage has ensued. Barricades and barriers have been destroyed but injury and death have been forestalled by Gerard's constant recounting of Camarguaise folk tales. Every time the horses taste the onset of the killing instinct, Gerard hauls them to their senses with a promise of the next chapter of their heritage. And all arrive safely, if slightly dishevelled, at the little arena that, even the tiniest of villages in these environs, is an obligatory element of the infrastructure. And you, dear unknowing reader, need fear not: it is forbidden in this part of the South to kill the bulls that run.

Among the many that have witnessed this event is a small female who nightly resides behind the PMU bar. Netty has located Monsieur Villiers once more and is questioning him with all the rigour of one who might have been mentored by the Spanish Inquisition. Monsieur Villiers, having finally understood that he is the prime suspect in Netty's search for a father, is sympathetic. He is charmed by the innocence of the barmaid's desire for familial fulfilment. He wishes desperately that he could help her; that he could be a missing and longed-for link in somebody's life. But he isn't. And it's futile to try to intertwine his life story with hers. Nothing fits and at last Netty realises that she has been beating a genetic path in the wrong direction. Nonetheless, these two have, from desperation and loss, forge some sort of bond and agree to sit with each other at the forthcoming communal dinner this evening.

It's a long hard slog under the too-hot-to-handle sun, even for those that failed to make an early start. Despite missing a church service to give thanks for, among other things, the subsequent opportunity to purchase other people's unwanted belongings at the also-neglected annual vide-grenier, all have managed to deal with the lunchtime aperitif. They have further participated in or simply observed les animaux in the streets of Cabannes. However, the day is far from over. Next on the agenda is the three hour spectacle of bull-baiting. This, naturally, will be followed by the evening aperitif that is a forerunner to the communal paella that, in turn, precedes dancing to the Johnny Hallyday tribute band. For some of our friends, this is all too exhausting. Largely, these comprise anyone who is not French or who are vegetarian animal lovers. Louise and assorted guests plus Phyllida and the partner who cannot be named leave for a little siesta under various trees in respective gardens; some in wooden Swedish chairs from which, later, they may have to be extricated. Everyone else makes their way to the arena for a refreshing bottle of beer or two.

Chapter Twenty~Eight

Reader, in other circumstances, you and I could also give the bull-ring a miss and retire quietly for a snooze in the shade. Bull-baiting is a spectacle that might be seen once in order that we can say we were there but it's not really suitable for your literary gentility. However, on this occasion, we need to make a transitory incursion into the arena to observe the non-animal participants so, for the novices among you, a brief contextualisation is required. A number of bulls, usually of the smaller variety, are, one by one, invited into the ring. Each of these animals has, beforehand, been garnished with ribbons between their ears or on their tiny horns. Young men of the razateur ilk then try to remove these decorations. Well, that's enough of the travel guide. Back to Netty and Gerard who are moving among the now horseless gardians.

Previously, Netty has had little contact with Gerard since that evening spent in the company of the mustard-clothed, wine-soaked rabbit when she attempted to question his provenance. However, having been inspired by the tiny horse whisperer's accomplishment of finding a father, she has secured herself to him and is currently being introduced to acquaintances from the Camargue. A number of others are also in this party. Monsieur Martin, having relinquished his equine fête duties, is expressing interest in the towering white horses that, similarly, have completed their responsibilities. In this he is, somewhat surprisingly, accompanied by his diminutive wife who seems, limpet-like, to have permanently attached herself to his arm. Their son is elsewhere in the arena surrounded by those who once comprised members of Team PMU and Team PMU2 and who will, in all likelihood, never do so again. It's irrelevant: they are busy drinking and shouting support to selected razateurs on whom an indiscriminate amount of euro has been placed. Madame Lapin is also close at hand on the raised wooden benches where she has been lately abandoned by the paella purveyor who has, ostensibly, left to prepare tonight's communal dinner. Except that, in reality, Jean-Pierre Lucard is currently in the coral stalking anybody else who might be in the jam and pickle business. Apart from a man from Chateaurenard who has been assigned the job of casting a well-being eye over bulls and horses, veterinary practitioners are conspicuous by their absence; although this doesn't mean that they aren't also in the vicinity on the lookout for opportunities of any kind.

Gerard is overwhelmed by many things this day. Predominately amongst these is the reunion with his father. A close second, was participating in the parade as a Gardian. In no particular order after these accomplishments was locating a number of the lads he'd grown up with in the mosquito-infested Camargue, the new friends he has made amongst the older men in the troupe and now the unexpected accessory comprised of a tiny woman who works behind the PMU bar. However, with regard to the last group of overwhelming interlopers, he is feeling – well, a little overwhelmed. Gerard is in the business of speaking soothingly to horses but now finds he has, inadvertently, assumed the role of bodyguard to Netty who appears to be the newly-found true love of every Gardian with or without a wife down in the Camargue. Gerard wonders where Christophe is.

Meanwhile, Madame Martin is not having the easiest of afternoons either. Temporarily freed from jam and pickle bondage, and having purposively misplaced her business partner, the lady from the bottom of the lane that runs away from everything is trying to restore something that may have not existed in the first place. Which is to say, that, this afternoon, she is sick to the back teeth of peaches, courgettes, onions and anything else in that field. She's had enough of off-the-shoulder and down-to-the-elbow fashions. She's temporarily done with markets and stalls. She's had sufficient experience in supervising young women to populate one hundred CVs. She might be able to manage another small aperitif but, in general, Madame Martin would just like to spend some quality time with her husband.

'Bonjour, darling', says an onion-scented man with silver locks who could have almost anyone he wants and therefore wants the person who is unavailable. 'I hope you will save a dance for me this evening.'

Monsieur Martin, busy looking up at the towering white horses in wonder, is momentarily preoccupied. Madame Martin strains her miniscule neck to look up at the not-so-silver-but-more-white-haired man, not in wonder. Madame Martin is French so, naturally, tries to be as polite as is humanly possible given her irritation, indifference and her singular dislike of paella purveyors. However, she is allotted insufficient time to construct, construe or even conjugate a suitable response because, not for the first time during this weekend, someone else has jumped out from behind a metaphorical lamp-post, although not with a view to frightening the horses:

'Is this person worrying you', enquires a hitherto missing person from south of the South? Madame Martin is further irritated and annoyed, this time by persons of veterinary proportions who are also presenting their symbolic dance-cards as if they are some kind of modern day Monsieur d'Arcy.

And Monsieur Martin, having finally experienced sufficient smallness for one lifetime, and an adequate dearth of aperitifs for one afternoon, deals with both of his wife's admirers in the traditional mode. To the great surprise of everyone, he kicks Jean-Pierre Lucard and Monsieur Villiers, one by one, in their respective, but not necessarily respectable, knee-caps.

Chapter Twenty-Nine

The crowds, soaked in the aperitif, have poured themselves into the car-park at Intermarché in almost liquid form. They are now busy fighting over their places at the benches in readiness for the communal paella. Villagers, with longer histories of unknown familial disputes than we might care to cope with, are squabbling politely. This one doesn't want to sit with that one. That one's grandmother once had a liaison with another one's third cousin, twice removed. The great niece of the third cousin, twice removed, is currently part of a ménage à trois involving an artisan boulanger and an electrician of dubious provenance. Naturally, the attainment of appropriate seating arrangements is further prolonged by the necessity of kissing all those who might want to be kissed, plus a bunch of also-rans who expect something wet on the cheek from anyone who's passing by. Small children attempt to kill each other between the supports of the trestle tables. The ex-pats have formed a mass of new solidarity at one end. The previous day's bonhomie has, apparently, dissipated and no-one of French origin wants to kiss anyone of non-French origin from St.Remy. With the possible exception of men from Orange with silver hair.

For the most part, those who have populated this story have managed to stay close to each other; although possibly not in each individual's preferred permutation. Monsieur Martin, having fought his way through the hand-shaking, kissing-anyone crowds, has now reappeared alongside his newly conjoined wife who, in turn, is adjacent to Sophy and an apparently exhausted Dr Giraud. Opposite, sit Christophe and Netty. The father-finding Gerard has taken his promised place on the other side of the yet-to-find-a-family young woman. Gerard was hoping to share a meal with his latterly-located papa but the gardians, celebrating the last gig of the season, are on a mission. They have split from their ranks in order to integrate in as many ways as are humanly possible. Phyllida and the partner who cannot be named, along with Louise, her lawn-mowing husband and various clients intent on completing this week's online table d'hôte ratings, have formed a cosmopolitan crowd in between the already seated diners. Clovis whines. But Clovis whines from an, as yet, unknown position somewhere under the tables.

Jean-Pierre Lucard is king of all he surveys. Cabannes may well be a no-one's-ever-heard-of-the-place type of village but JPL has, one way and another, had a very successful weekend in these tiny streets. It's true he's nursing a pair of badly bruised kneecaps but they are carefully hidden under his pristine blue jeans. It's also the case that women adept in the jam-making business may not have been as keen as they could be in the try-anything-once department. On the other hand, librarians wearing roses have more than made up for pickle purveyors under the influence of those with small spotted ponies. Plus the silver-haired man has more options than he cares to count amongst the party-holding ex-pats. And the night is young; possibly more so than those in charge of the paella.

Other people with bruised knees are keeping themselves to themselves. The last bus back to Plan d'Orgon, if it ever existed, left long ago but the once-romantic-hero, who latterly moved to the role of duplicitous interloper, has, once again, been abandoned by all and sundry. Well, nearly all. Dogs that were once wolves have finally developed a long memory. Unknown to most present, one of this breed is now lying quietly, for the time being, at the feet of persons of a veterinary bent who can speak in canine tongues. However, just as Monsieur Villiers is mulling over the unfairness of life, his partner in crime arrives to take a somewhat reluctant seat at his side. Madame Lapin is not a happy woman and is seriously considering a move to fifth wave feminism. Having followed and adapted the younger generation's ideals of keeping all options open, she has, at last, recognised a sad truth: there aren't quite as many options to open or close in maturity. Abandoned in the bull-ring by the paella purveyor and temporarily discarded by her business partner, the librarian has discovered that visitors from Plan d'Orgon might represent her last-ditch saloon if she is not to be seen socialising alone. She shuffles into her place on the bench whereupon her feet make contact with an unknown entity under the table. Madame Lapin attempts to kick the irritating unknown entity out of the way. A strange growl-like noise emanates from between the trestles. Madame Lapin assumes this to be the horrid children intent on mutual infanticide below and draws her high-heeled shoes beneath her seat in some discomfort.

Chapter Thirty

It's impossible for anyone, regardless of temperament, to complain about the dinner. The French know how to do these things without trying. Obviously, there is an aperitif. Reader, you might by now have surmised that 'the aperitif' is a generic term used to describe any form of liquid refreshment that arrives any time before any meal. Actually, it can even replace the meal as in the apero dinatoire whereupon large amounts of alcohol are consumed throughout the evening to the accompaniment of a range of small cold edibles. It's quite a nice way for the hostess, and never a host, to get through a night of social discourse without having to cook anything; although the preparation is tedious: all those floral carrots are enough to drive a person to extremes. Tonight, however, there will be dinner so the aperitif comprises bottles of rosé from south of the South, generously distributed along the white linen clothed tables. After this, and to the accompaniment of the heady red wines of the Rhône Valley, our diners are visited by the cold meats and enormous juicy tomatoes so evocative of the south. In subsequent years, this course will also comprise the jars of peach jelly which will, eventually, make small fortunes for the two bonnes madames and will be celebrated in local history and recipe books designed for unwitting tourists.

Next, plates of green beans sprinkled with garlic and lemon arrive to purify the blood. Then there is a pause in proceedings. In truth, there is a pause in proceedings between all courses in a French meal to ensure adequate conversation and lubrication. Were we to indulge and investigate all these pauses in a literary manner, we might be here for several extra and unnecessary chapters. Nonetheless, in the pause between the green beans and the arrival of the paella, there is a transfer of seating arrangements. Christophe leaves his place on the bench, firstly to speak with Papa and Maman. His place, next to Netty, is immediately taken by a person new to these pages. One of the more enthusiastic gardians, Philippe, as if awaiting life-changing opportunities, slides into his newly allotted position and begins to engage Netty in small talk. But Philippe's small talk is of potentially greater proportions. By the time the bean course plates are being cleared, and the twice-used cutlery is silently waiting the new challenges provided by Jean-Pierre Lucard, Netty has been alerted to the fact that the middle-aged Philippe has an equine-related history originating in Marseilles. However, just as the barmaid is about to enquire after new leads, two important things happen: firstly, some people begin to be served with the paella. Secondly, there is an altercation at that part of the communal bench which involves wolves with memories and vets who speak in forked tongues.

Christophe, under the influence of the bonhomie induced by the rosé from south of the South, and several other alcoholic beverages, is pleased to see some sort of limpet-like reunion between his parents. He has now decided to make sure the evening ends well, before it has barely begun, by finally sorting out Monsieur Villiers. It's yet another grudge match which Christophe is determined to win; although, this time, without recourse to general knowledge. The handshakes, 'bonsoirs', 'meh bahs' and 'mais ouis', as a matter of protocol between the two, are dealt with and disposed of almost before Monsieur Villiers has time to consider his options. Any further consideration time is terminated by a left hook received politely on his right cheek. Monsieur Villiers, surrounded by a sudden and unexpected shower of lemon and garlic-covered green bean leftovers, subsequently acknowledges his options as somewhat limited.

And that might be the end of this unfortunate interlude was it not for the fact that a dog who was once a wolf has finally located his long-term memory. From this black hole that contains cages, ropes, blue fur, domicile and visiting lady dogs, policemen and firefighters, ponies, parades and neighbours and men who cannot be named, Clovis delves further into the unknown. He arrives at a point where a drunken potato-packer who has won ownership of a nameless puppy, leaves him to rot amongst the overgrown rhubarb at the bottom of a lane that could be anywhere. Clovis moves slightly forward along this dark chasm and finds a small vet from south of the South who speaks kindly and, in many ways, releases him from a life of confinement. And from his resting place beneath the trestle tables, Clovis puts one and one together and, surprisingly, makes two. Using his newly-discovered, critically analytical skills, he weighs up the pros and cons of Monsieur Villiers and the potato packer and reaches a conclusion; which is to say, Clovis decides to kill Christophe.

Chapter Thirty~One

Other people have simultaneously reached important milestones in their lives: Monsieur and Madame Martin, whose life changes and continuations have, let's face it, underpinned this story, have rediscovered some things that they may have known all along. In no particular order, they have looked along the tables at their family, their friends and their neighbours and decided that they live lives that are far from the insular existences they had taken for granted. They have looked up at the Provençal night sky, in which the reliable sun is setting for another day, and agreed that there is, in all probability, nowhere better to pass a lifetime. And they have also looked at each other and are, frankly, amazed at the accomplishments of each. Louise and the lawn-mowing husband, Phyllida and the partner, who cannot be named, also regard each other closely as the lightest of evening breezes momentarily stirs their thoughts of home. They are ex-pats of a different variety to those from St Remy; which is to say, there is no sense of transience in their existence. They have created new lives along the road that runs from Noves to Cabannes and with regard to this decision, they are terminally happy. They are home.

On the other hand, as the song of the cicadas dies until tomorrow, and the owls emerge to take their places, those also considering their lives have important decisions to make. Madame Lapin has possibly undergone more changes than anyone else throughout these pages. Well, more changes of clothes at least! There have been refutations of life-long ideology, a discovery of men that has necessitated a consideration of the benefits and disadvantages of at least two of this species, a diversification away from all things literary into the world of fashion, and, of course, an introduction to the world of business. From a distance, she looks at Madame Martin and in an awareness of some irony, Madame Lapin realises that the most satisfying change she has undergone is that in which she has discovered a female friend.

Sophy, meanwhile, has, for the time being, recognised that, by playing her cards carefully, she can have both Dr Giraud and the opportunity to spend time down that lane we have come to know so well. There's no current hope of change for either Christophe or Jean-Pierre Lucard but this in itself is a resolution of sorts: we can know nothing if we fail to know ourselves. And that leaves the minor protagonists, Netty and Philippe. Ironically, their milestone is possibly the greatest this evening. Amongst the bonhomie, the freely flowing wine, the superb food and all things French, it is these two who have enjoyed the most demanding and inquisitive, but side-lined, of conversations. Now, it transpires that it's more than likely they are, in some way, related. And when we say 'in some way', we mean in the closest of ways: for there is no getting away from the fact that, finally, and quite by the serendipity forged by seating arrangements, Netty has found her father.

Thus, as we draw this evening, this meal and this story to a close, we might suitably leave Cabannes, and the roads running to and from, at a point where most people have resolved most things as far as possible in a life where some sort of future can only be assumed. Except that, there's that business with a wolf, a vet and an academic potato packer. Under the darkening skies and the growing moon, which, in both this story and reality, is the only thing that is truly larger than life, the paella plates and seats of the many are upturned: Clovis finally seeks vengeance, retribution and justice for all the many earlier sufferings of his doggy life. Christophe, for his troubles, receives an unpleasant set of canine canines on his knee; which means at least three people present are unable to walk without the attendance of sticks. Jean-Pierre Lucard, who happens to be delivering two plates of paella at a near-at-hand juncture, suffers secondary injuries to his pristine blue jeans. Fortuitously, the shiny buckled belt that holds the essentials in place is undamaged. Madame Lapin rushes to the aid of both of the men in her fantasy life and from a loudspeaker Kalman Aleksander and his band initiate the entrée to the Johnny Hallyday tribute act. Which cheers the partner who cannot be named no end.

And speaking of ends, a story has to finish somewhere even if the end is not really the final instalment. Some folk are badly bruised but no-one has died. Actually, with a bit of luck, that last sentence could be applied to almost anyone's story. But not everyone's story takes place in the south of France. Not all stories close with all the participants dancing to a Johnny Hallyday tribute band under night-time skies lit by shooting stars. Not every protagonist will wake in other stories knowing there's no need to draw back the curtains in order to see what the day has delivered. Lives which don't involve semi-naked tractor drivers and women who become pickle purveyors are, for the large part irrelevant. This is because the lives of the ordinary are always extraordinary. Clovis whines.

Le Fin

(for the time being)

If you enjoyed this book, please let Madame Verte know. She currently lives in Dorset where she also writes under the name of Alison Green: aligreen52@hotmail.com

17914581R00079

Printed in Poland
by Amazon Fulfillment
Poland Sp. z o.o., Wrocław